I0518583

Antiphon

Antiphon

*A Call and Response
in a Year of
Grief and Renewal*

Jane Flynn ~ Christina Holbrook

FIRST EDITION

All rights reserved, including the right of reproduction in whole or in part in any form. No part of this book may be used or reproduced in any manner for the purpose of training artificial intelligence technologies or systems.

Copyright© 2025 by Jane Flynn and Christina Holbrook

Published by Ikaros Books
New York, NY

Manufactured in the United States of America

Paperback ISBN   979-8-9993628-0-3

E-book ISBN   979-8-9993628-1-0

Library of Congress Control Number: 2025918316

Cover art by Mara L. Flynn

Cover and interior design by Ashley Prine, Tandem Books

*For Alan
and
for Greg*

Preface

We have been friends for forty-five years. Although our lives have followed very different trajectories, and we've mostly moved in separate circles of acquaintances, we share commonalities of experience from growing up in the same East Coast town and attending the same college. We came of age together during a period of great social transition for women, with a similar eagerness to learn, to succeed at work, to love and to experience the world.

Our orbits first intersected long ago during these formative years in the 1970s and 1980s, and then again nearly four decades later when time and experience had reshaped both of our lives. Chris had moved from the East Coast to Breckenridge, Colorado, and embarked on her third marriage after years of tumultuous personal relationships. Jane was navigating her separation after twenty-five years of marriage, facing the challenge of shifting into life as a single expat woman in Greece.

Our affinity for one another's stories and approaches to life blossomed as we reconnected. But before long, the recent, hard-won stability of our lives was shaken, first by the death of Jane's twenty-two-year-old son Greg by suicide and then by Chris' implacable diagnosis of terminal brain cancer. All at once, each of us became trapped in a state of mourning—inertia, sadness, and loss made it impossible to discern a path forward. *What if*, Chris suggested, *we try writing to one another?* About what we are going through, about anything, really. Just write.

Even before we began this correspondence, we'd talked together about the phenomenon of people distancing themselves, consciously or not, from each of us in the wake of our personal tragedies. It's a profoundly human response, and Western culture is rife with none-too-reassuring examples of friends, families, and communities turning away from those hapless individuals whose lives have been upended by a chance meeting with fate.

When God decides to inflict the most horrific trials on his faithful servant, everyone around Job scatters. The innocent victims of the Greek gods, subject to the brutal whims of those who feel only desires and are heedless of consequences, are similarly abandoned by family and friends racing to get themselves out of the line of divine fire.

Sometimes, that distancing comes from a sense of inadequacy in the face of stark tragedy: *How can I possibly help or make this better? I can't imagine what this person is going through (nor can I bear to). I'll just avoid the topic and the person.*

But for us, avoidance was not and is not an option. Jane had to confront the unbearable sight of her child in a drawer in a hospital morgue; Chris stood frozen and uncomprehending as her physician husband read her first MRI results and wept.

To survive what in the darkest moments seems unsurvivable, we've learned that we must have people in our lives ready to bear witness with us. Family, friends or neighbors who call, knit blankets, or sew quilts, send favorite books or meals. People who check in gently, listen without judgment. These have not always been the people that we expected, but they have been the friends we need, offering the extraordinary gifts of their generosity and steadfastness.

Important in a different way is having someone to turn to who is experiencing a similarly bleak and inescapable reality. That person gets it; they know the suffering we are confronting won't "get better," that we won't wake up to find it was all a terrible nightmare, that there are no miracles. We have become, for each other, the witness who walks beside you.

We have loved these months of corresponding with each other for the simple yet life-affirming feeling of having someone to walk with in the deep woods. Writing has affected us both minutely and profoundly. The words we write can't change what *is*, but they have made it more bearable. Most of our writing is straightforward, but we've also shared poems, fantasy, and flights of imagination. Having this sacred space in which to write about our grief in the context of lives that go on, grow, and bring joy and gratitude, along with the pain and moments of desolation, makes it easier for each of us to find hope and purpose.

If we have anything to offer the world, it's the honest conversation of two friends as we try to find ways to live lives of meaning while also waking each day to the ongoing experience of terrible loss. Our writing meanders. Sometimes, we address the specific trauma that moved us to write, but just as often, we reflect on what we are reading, doing, and thinking, and the people and experiences that have helped to shape us into the women we are today.

We did not set out to create anything more than the conversation between us, but we've come to believe that our conversation could resonate with others. If this is so, then that is grace.

Christina and Jane,
August 2025

The worst thing and the best thing is that I can't be angry with you, can't summon any emotion other than love, wounded love, like you had peeled strips of my skin. Pain and love. You are my beautiful boy, my strong, my solid Gregos.

Jane, August 2021, *journal entry*

In the slow-motion time after surgery, I watched the moon's gentle passage, and it filled me with peace. I drifted away from the world of the living: So that's that. I am dying. But my otherwise healthy body reasserted itself. My mind cleared. Now, I am filled with rage and an unbearable sense of loss.

Chris, April 2022, *journal entry*

Beginning the Conversation

November 12, 2022
Breckenridge, Colorado

I PULL ON MY BOOTS and follow the logging road behind the house as it climbs the open hillside, then continues on into the woods. I take the same walk almost every day. The repetition never bothered or bored me as I was inside my own head, distracted by an ever-changing cascade of thoughts, images, and mundane preoccupations. Once, my mind might have jumped from a story I was working on to lunch plans with my husband to fretting over when I was going to tackle the decluttering project in my clothes closet and file drawers. I might hardly have noticed my rugged exterior surroundings.

Today, I scramble down a trail to a pool that is hidden from the dirt road. My eyes search this scant bit of water: near the center, at the very bottom of the pool, a bubbling up of sand reveals an underground spring. This is what I want to see. "Sacred spring," I murmur to myself and watch the pulse and swirl of water as if willing it to offer me a sign of hope. In this arid terrain, the life-sustaining spring is a small, determined miracle—like a flame flickering and pushing back the dark in a world that has become, for me, cloaked in dread.

Everything changed after I received the results of the MRI scan of my brain in March of this year. The test had been ordered following a series of strange visual disturbances. My doctor, my husband, and I had been unconcerned, confident that this test was probably unnecessary; surely the symptoms were due to ocular migraines. We were wrong.

On April 8, 2022, I had surgery to remove a tumor from the right occipital lobe of my brain, diagnosed as a grade-four glioblastoma. The median life expectancy for patients like me, my surgeon and neuro-oncologist told me only after asking if this was information I wanted to know, is fourteen to twenty-two months. Hands in my lap in the doctor's office, I counted on my fingers: I have until sometime between May 2023 and January 2024.

Now, I do not want to focus on what is going on inside my head—literally or figuratively. But I need to walk. Only these days I concentrate on seeing outside of myself as if this will help make sense of what is happening to me. How do I fit into this world around me? Is there any purpose to this life that I am moving through suddenly, much too quickly? Around a bend and further up the logging road, a path leads off into the woods. I take this and eventually emerge onto a wide overlook with the Colorado mountains, capped in early snow, sweeping out before me.

Maybe I am hoping for a broader view, a sense of perspective, and yet right now, I look around and struggle to see where my place is, or has ever been for that matter.

As I begin down the switchback trail, wary of ice under last night's snow, my mind backslides into fear-filled chatter. Then, a sound overhead catches my attention, stops me. I can't quite place the noise but know it is from some kind of bird. It is a great "klack-klack-klack" mixed with a loud screeching.

I stand on the hillside where sage and small wild rose bushes huddle under a cold sky, and snow crystals gust through the air. The noise above anchors me in time: late fall—the season of long journeys. I look up, and I see the sandhill cranes, a dozen maybe, high above me. Their long legs drift behind them as they fly in a slow circle, their voices crying out to one another. I know that they will meet up with others, creating bigger circles in the air, and then, in one mysterious moment, that circle will unwind. Individual groups of birds will peel off instinctively and fly together south.

I fumble for my phone to take a picture. When I look up again, they are gone. Gone! I wanted to see them circling one more time! I wanted to take one snapshot that would capture this strange, beautiful ritual like a certainty. But there is no certainty. Everything comes down to chance, doesn't it? How will all the cranes survive the journey that lies ahead? It is so cold and even colder up in that late November sky. Some will surely die. When I come off the trail, I am drenched in inexplicable grief.

I want to know: *Why?*

Why were we all made so beautiful and so fragile? Why made to have a sense of purpose, toward which we fly? Or voices that call to each other or beating wings?

Thank you for reading these words,
Chris

November 14, 2022
New York, New York

I WALK THROUGH THE PARK to be alone, to observe the masses of humans sharing the space but living different things. At this point, I know the paths through New York's Central Park almost by feel; my internal GPS plots my route from home to the park depending on where I cross 5th Avenue to avoid waiting for the light. The Manhattan sport of jaywalking, where it's a point of pride never to wait at an intersection if possible, is ingrained, and the momentary pleasure of seamless striding is part of why I walk.

There are rare moments of fleeting human connection, like the Tuesday morning when a tawny hawk flew close overhead above the reservoir and settled on a branch right above the path. One young couple dove for their phones to take photos; another couple, closer to me in age, smiled with me conspiratorially in that fleeting New York acknowledgement of shared experience. I stayed, watching the hawk for a few more minutes, perhaps hoping that its air of calm control would impart some sense of balance.

I don't stop to think if I am observed, even as I slot the people I see into transient mental categories. Northern European tourists wrestling with unfolded maps, the mother patient, the father intent, the gawky teen children wavering between curiosity and boredom; two women in their early forties, fit as racehorses in Lululemon, with matching blonde ponytails threaded through the baseball caps emblazoned with their law firm's name, their pace matched by the intensity of their conversation; an old man in a wheelchair with motionless, gnarled, spotted hands folded atop the blanket covering his legs, sitting next to his aide, a young Asian man with a kind face; an African immigrant kneeling, his prayer rug spread over crisp, fallen leaves.

It's my drug of choice, this daily walking. I weave in between slower walkers, maintaining a steady, aerobically challenging pace, listening to a podcast as I choose the daily variations in my path while observing the other park visitors. I can control this one thing, and my day is ordered by it. For these two hours, I can avoid thinking about the big existential question of who I am and what I want.

I know that I no longer can hold certain that I will find joy and purpose now that grief limns every thought, every reaction. I spent most of the past year finishing the newly urgent checklists of things I had to accomplish in my reinvention as a New Yorker. Grief-fueled anger and fear spurred me through divorce and the dismantling of the thirty years of my life in Greece. I am starting to settle my raw roots in a new place that I hope will be permanent.

But what still evades me is peace, a sense that this move toward permanence will bring the resolution I had hoped for without realizing that was my goal. It unsettles me, the sense that I am failing at something, that I should have figured out by now what to want. How to want. I do not *need*, but I should *want*, right?

Other walks remind me starkly of how privileged I am not to need. Madison Avenue, after nine p.m., is marked by the barely intrusive presence of those who need. Their cardboard shelters are set up in boutique doorways where they seek safety while telegraphing vulnerability. I wonder what the calculus of fear must be. I feel guilty that I have such security but no peace.

I have a photo over my desk of one of the last times I felt truly whole. I am seated on the beach, my beach, between my two boys, in August of 2020. We're together, a rare enough event when my oldest lives so far away and all the more precious because of the pandemic that makes travel so difficult and perilous. There is nothing more I want in that moment but to savor the sunset with them before going back to the house and cooking dinner for them, watching them splash in the pool and joke with their friends.

I am angry with myself for not knowing how precious this would be, for not paying more attention to every detail, for letting it be ordinary. I will not have that ordinary ever again. Is that why, instead of trying to find beauty and purpose in each day, I choose to experience life through mute observation? Can I avoid further pain if I fail to choose anything to care about?

But this city is where I have chosen to be at home, and sometimes it is enough. The Canada geese on the rowboat lake call to mind Mary Oliver's poem "Wild Geese": "Tell me about despair, yours, and I will tell you mine." I am still finding my place in the family of things.

Talk soon,
Jane

November 18, 2022
Breckenridge, Colorado

Today, as I hike up the mountain, I circle back to this thought: Maybe I am hoping for a broader view, a sense of perspective, and yet right now, I look around and struggle to see where my place is or has ever been for that matter.

The diagnosis of terminal brain cancer is so nightmarish, so utterly incomprehensible, it both numbs me and drives me forward with a kind of terror-filled urgency. All the questions I thought I still had some vague notion of "the rest of my life" to figure out must be answered *now*.

And perhaps your description of the photo, of the last time you felt whole, is what sends me in from the trail through the woods and up to a corner of our upstairs bedroom to study a photo from my childhood. I have rarely looked at it in these past years, but now, when I hold the small gilded frame, the image behind the glass fills me with longing and sorrow, questions without answers, and something I will—now—never experience again: the memory of what it was like to feel safe.

You held our hands, Dad, in this golden-hued, fifty-year-old photo of my sister and me taken on a dirt road beneath the New Hampshire fall foliage. Walking ahead, the photographer—my mother—captured the three of us skipping towards her. My father was so handsome. Trim and blond and wearing pressed gray trousers and a white

Oxford shirt, he appeared as formal as a prep school teacher as he drew our gazes to his raised right knee: *Like this.*

My sister and I, scruffier in our jeans but with rapt expressions, studied his movement, trying to copy it. Each of us had our right leg raised, poised for skipping. I must have been ten and my sister seven (our infant brother at home with a babysitter); presumably, we knew how to skip. But as I study this photo now, it occurs to me that what my father was teaching us was how to skip *together*, as a group, father and daughters—as a family.

And because my serious dad had a goofy, playful side, too, he was likely chanting "Lions and tigers and bears!" from *The Wizard of Oz* movie, repeating the phrase faster and faster, egging us on. Soon, my father, sister, and I were filling that far-off afternoon with excited shouts of "Lions and tigers and bears! Oh, my!" My mother ran ahead of us, turning to snap photos, pictures so lovely they could have been on a postcard or a magazine cover, advertising the wonders of New England.

It was many years later that I came across this old photo tucked into a file folder of grade school short stories, report cards, and hand-made valentines. On a visit home—my parents still lived in the house by the school on Edgewood Road, where we'd grown up—I'd pulled the photo out of my bag to surprise my father.

In his midseventies, age had made him somehow pensive and withdrawn, less apt to laugh. I was fifty. I felt certain the photo would please him and bring back happy memories and a smile. "Look what I found!" I said, handing the Kodak snapshot to my father as we sat at the kitchen table. He lifted his eyeglasses from his nose and squinted at the small photo. His face flushed, and he teared up. Almost immediately, my confidence turned to dread; I had done something wrong. My father, the self-controlled, soft-spoken lawyer, with that natural restraint and sense of propriety, began to cry.

"Dad? What's wrong?"

"This photo . . ." He cleared his throat. "It just reminds me of my . . . responsibilities."

I didn't know what to do. In a family that rarely allowed for the vulnerability of sharing complicated personal feelings, I was taken off guard by his obvious distress. I turned my uncertainty inward: *How stupid of me! Insensitive. Why wasn't I better at reading my father's mood?* I slid the snapshot back into my bag as he got up from the table.

Today, that photo of a happy, long-ago afternoon sits on a table in my guest room. It's as if I'd placed it somewhere that is visible but where I wouldn't have to confront the image—and my inability to fully understand my father or our relationship—too often. However, in the past few months, the desire to know has become more urgent. I need to put order to the various fragments of my own life, like piecing together a collage of random pictures that will miraculously take a form that makes sense to me. And so, I study the photo again.

Am I asking for the impossible by insisting that any two people could truly know one another? Perhaps parents and children are particularly mysterious to each other, because it is hard for me to imagine that my father needed to be reminded of his responsibilities. He was such a responsible father and husband. Über responsible.

Had he meant to say *burden*? Were we a burden, we who were his responsibility? It saddens me to think this. And I am sadder still for never having asked so that I could have understood my father's fears, regrets, and satisfactions—glimpsed more clearly what he really felt. And shared with him how I felt. Because two years after I showed my father that photo, he died.

There is something that I want to say to my father. As I take in the young faces that still brighten this faded snapshot and the country setting that is genuine and imperfect, not some slick modern Instagram posting, my eyes blur. I hear the faint music of laughter. I know exactly what it was like to be part of our long-ago family, with parents who loved each other and loved their three children. Caught forever in this photo and in my heart is the joy of having known those moments—of having experienced family outings filled with silliness and delight and days stretching into a future to look forward to.

And now, as I face down more fearsome lions and tigers and bears at this late and uncertain time in my life, *I still remember how safe I once felt, Dad, when you held my hand.*

Chris

November 26, 2022
New York, New York

W E HAD GOOD DADS, CHRIS. The photo I see every time I open my laptop was taken the week before my fiftieth birthday, on the beach. I am embraced by my parents, each of us in hoodies or sweaters against the late-October cool. At the time, I thought the photo was proof of how blessed I was to have both of them healthy as friends and parents. We watched the sun sink into the sea, then turned back to the house, its broad veranda glowing as the setting sun reddened the terra cotta color of the rough-plastered exterior. Safety and security with my family.

Over the next month, I would make two hurried visits to Amagansett, the last extended to accommodate Dad's wake and funeral, the shockingly swift collapse of his health still not registering fully. During my first visit, when most of us gathered for a grimly upbeat Thanksgiving dinner, he was unable to eat, his skin visibly yellowed; Dad still had the energy to tell me about one of the last surgeries he performed. A young man had been bench-pressing weights, his spotter's attention wandered, and the bar had come down on his throat, neatly severing his trachea without breaking the skin. The complication was that the patient was also a singer, and a simple repair sufficient to let him breathe could leave him with a scarred trachea that might affect his vocal cords. The OR nurses trusted Dad's judgment when he spent twice as long as the repair strictly required, patiently and meticulously repairing the damaged tissue with minute stitches, a cosmetic-level repair that would remain invisible but crucial for the young man's future.

I realized that my father was telling me who he was as a surgeon, not only as my father. I knew his deft hands could make furniture, nurture bonsai, and repair the cuts and scrapes of grandchildren. I was honored that he shared this story with me and saddened to know that it meant he knew he had limited time to share the legacy of his identity.

I returned to Greece for a brief trip last week to attend my final General Assembly as a board member and officer of the Mediterranean Garden Society. (As with many small organizations, the absence of significant issues seems to engender intense emotions over ridiculously trivial matters, so I had to show up in person.) It was a difficult week—being in Athens brought forth so many memories and entangled parts of my identity.

I felt like an alien, an outsider, in places where I had lived, walked, shopped, and worked for over thirty years. Most of the shops were just as I left them two years ago, and my feet knew where to turn. I navigated Athens's tangled grid in my friend's car without thinking, steering effortlessly into familiar shortcuts and back streets. I remembered where to find good parking, where to stand on the metro platforms, and how to move quickly from the train platform to Monastiraki Square to Lysiou Street. But while I felt like an intruder, an imposter, this unease didn't seem to be visible to the friends I saw. In addition to those I planned to see, I ran into acquaintances by chance, their eyes widening with surprise and sincere pleasure. So why was I so uncomfortable?

Other images came to mind after a sad, short lunch with my former husband, who I have decided to refer to as my "wasband." I had asked him for a separation after twenty-five years of marriage, the last five spent in optimistic but fruitless attempts to establish an effective dialogue, but we didn't proceed to divorce until after Greg died, and I had moved to New York. This was the man I had loved for over twenty years, in whom I had placed my trust, the man for whom I moved halfway around the world, for whom I left my home, family, and culture, the father of my two children. This was also the man whose younger son called him "the final nail in the coffin" in his suicide note.

He was waiting for me at the restaurant—he "didn't want to be late." He had been chronically late for most of our marriage, and his inability to see why I experienced that as evidence of his lack of regard for me had been a sullen bone of contention for at least the last ten years. Somewhat ironically, I saw his promptness now as evidence of his vulnerability. I found that I did not hate him, as I had a year ago, and realized that he no longer had the capacity to bully me. He was small. I could not conjure up the memory of how I had loved him, had smiled when I saw him, had delighted in sharing children with him. I ran out of things to say.

I grew restless, and he grew needy, rising from his seat to press next to me on the short bench, his arm around me without invitation. He seemed so diminished, stale somehow—I sat unmoving, patted his hand, and gently extricated myself as soon as I could do so kindly.

So many things are not what they seem to be. A photo of a perfect moment that actually chronicled imminent death, a place where I once belonged but that no longer feels like home, a person I knew as my own skin who has become a stranger.

I have decided to frame the acknowledgment of the impermanence of reality as a liberating refrain: "For now." This is how I feel, for now. This is what I experience, for now. This is where I belong, for now. Maybe it's the very fragility of reality that imbues it with value. I still see my father's arm around my shoulder at sunset on a beloved beach and smile.

Love,
Jane

Winter

December 1, 2022
Breckenridge, Colorado

Every two months, I undergo an MRI scan of my brain to detect any changes since my surgery in April and radiation treatments in May and June. My next scan is in a few days, and I am scared.

While I can remember, viscerally, the safety I felt as a very young child, especially around my dad, at the same time I am glad my parents are no longer around. The anguish they would have felt at my diagnosis is more than I can bear to imagine. Despite our sometimes tumultuous relationship, I know my parents loved me that much.

Last month, I sat in the neuro-oncology office with Alan on one side and the heavy bag of medications I now drag around with me everywhere on the other: Keppra for seizures, the nausea-inducing chemo drug TMZ, Valtrex to control outbreaks of cold sores due to my weakened immune system, Valium for anxiety, Colace for the constipation that is a result of all the previously mentioned drugs.

I asked Dr. Ney, "How long will I have to keep doing these brain scans?"

He answered, "At least two years." Dr. Ney, neuro-oncologist at University of Colorado Hospital, is kind and exactly as direct with me as I am with him—no more and no less.

Therefore, I did not ask him, "What happens after two years?" because then I might have been forced to hear him tell me: "You are not expected to live beyond two years."

At home, I have a table that holds an array of small objects collected over the years: shells, dried flowers, feathers, cedarwood, and sage, which I sometimes burn for the aromatic and cleansing smoke. Favorite stones evoke animal magic: a green stone for snake and transformation, a black stone speckled with silver mica for fearless jaguar, blue and orange for small-but-mighty hummingbird whose path leads to life's sweetness, and a gray-white stone for visionary eagle.

Among the objects on the table is a circular cast-metal belt buckle that was a prized possession of mine when I was a young teenager. The pewter disc holds the image of a woman's face—a woman warrior—her expression lit by a fiery war cry, hair streaming back beneath her winged helmet, a sword held high. She is not afraid.

Now, it is nighttime or early morning, I am not sure. I am so sick with fear and dread of the upcoming MRI that sleep has vanished, leaving me wide awake. I climb the stairs and go to this table with its objects that call to my imagination. The woman warrior gleams on the pewter buckle. *She is not afraid.* She is confronting whatever terror stands in front of her with a fierce cry, with all of her might. I pick up the metal piece, and slide my fingers over its cool surface. She tells me a story that is hers and mine:

> *I was born in a thundercloud above a rocky shore upon which the seas broke and narrow pines stood tall; their crowns pierced the sky. Lightning crashed; a sword fell into my open hands. I roped a wild horse with a moonbeam and galloped among the stars of the Milky Way.*
>
> *One day, my curiosity led me to the city, but I did not like to fold my wings beneath a suit, nor retract my sharp talons inside of high-heeled pumps. Some men thought I was a tame bird; I ate them for dinner, dropping their bones from the rooftop of my building. Then, a vision of flames warned me: go.*

Safe in the jungle, I slithered up into the arms of trees. What naps I had! What dreams! My mind played with stories, and my body shifted among many shapes until wilder lands called my name, and I journeyed as a shadow with four paws and sharp teeth. Beneath solemn mountains, I met a magician who cast a spell, hoping to stop time.

But thunder rumbles now, and my sword hums awake. I cannot sleep, the wild horse of the moon returns. The battle is coming.

I am ready.

May we be warrior women,
Chris

December 3, 2022
New York, New York

A S I CONTEMPLATED THE GIFT of friendship, my meditation app prompted me to focus on the moments of kindness and connection. From a smile between strangers to a classmate's phone call, an exchange of Instagram memes that say "I thought of you," the major and minor interactions that soften the edges of the day. On the morning that I was to go meet my wasband in Greece, you had sent me a photo of your bold, unafraid, determined woman warrior, whose spirit is embodied in the exuberant, consciously exultant battle cry she inspired in you. It was as though you knew just what to say to me to give me strength for the meeting. I hope she provides you with the same comfort that she did to me.

Coincidences can reinforce either the pessimistic or the hopeful, and a lot may depend on how the days spill into one another. Shortly after I got back from Greece, I spent a day with my friend Harriet and one of her good friends at the Thierry Mugler exhibition at the Brooklyn Museum.

Harriet was initially friends with my ex whom she had met when they were in law school together. We now joke that when sides were taken, I kept her in the divorce, and she is one of my steadfast friends in New York. She embodies generosity in action—she picked me up from a late-night arrival at Newark Airport back in 2017, when my older son Yannis was hospitalized with septic appendicitis, and drove him to the same airport to take the flight to Athens for Greg's funeral. I am blessed to have her in my life. And Greg knew her and loved her too.

At the exhibition, we took in the aesthetic of the 1970s to the 1990s, the juxtaposition of cutting-edge fashion brilliance and messages that now seem cruel, misogynistic, and dehumanizing. The most perceptive commentary in the exhibition noted that Mugler "did not objectify women, he subjectified them." We debated whether his treatment of women as Amazons—otherworldly, powerful sex goddesses—empowered or caricatured them, and, by extension, us. The undercurrents of drag queen and bondage culture, the metamorphosis of women into butterflies, sleek metallic robots, motorcycles—dizzying and disquieting, but undeniably beautiful. And what a joy to spend a day with bright women, mothers of daughters, discussing how we feel about women as we age, as we watch our children mature, the limits of invitation, consent, desire, sublimation, control—all the big issues that the show evoked.

I do not feel bold or strong, but I do feel fortunate. I am surrounded and buoyed by people who see me, know me, want to share thoughts and fears and joys and absurdities, who push me gently, with the faintest nudge of warm, soft fingers, to look at the light.

I found a joyously ridiculous paean to self, "Two Very Enthusiastic Thumbs Up," by one Ashley Rush, while wandering through the wilds of online content, that begins with the lines:

Today I will be my own best critic
I will give myself 5 stars just for showing up

and ends with the line:

10 out of 10 [I] would be me again.

Yes, I would be me again. Even to do it all over again. I would not forego knowing the people I lost. I would still fail to protect my heart and believe for too long in the wrong people, but I would want to experience all the joy and connection, even knowing the cost.

Love,
Jane

December 9, 2022
Breckenridge, Colorado

I RECALL WRITING A LETTER to *Vogue* as a high school student in the 1970s, protesting a piece that the magazine had run with photos by Helmut Newton, who was the photographer for several of Thierry Mugler's fashion campaigns. Newton's images were meant to be provocative and sexy; they were all about power and domination. I was sixteen or seventeen and asserted to the editors that Newton's leather-clad women subjects did not seem empowered to me, but rather packaged for the eyes of men! It is also possible that the fierce sexuality and the ambiguity of some of these images scared me at that age. Was that what I was supposed to want? To dress in black leather or latex? To crouch in submission or crack a whip?

Years later, in the 1990s, as head of The Black Book, a publishing company that produced directories of commercial advertising photography, I became extremely accustomed to seeing these sorts of images (not surprisingly, almost always the work of a male photographer). About a third of my New York City wardrobe at that time was leather; 100 percent of my wardrobe was black. And as the boss, I did a lot of whip-cracking.

This has been a week filled with both tremendous relief and great sadness.

The MRI scan of my brain came back with no sign of tumor regrowth. My immediate reaction was a mash-up of emotion: tears of relief, fighting with Alan, wanting to throw things across the room out of rage from the buildup of anxiety and pure terror. Finally, succumbing to forty-eight hours of sleep. When I awoke (two days later), it was with a renewed sense of hope, gratitude even, that I had been given the gift of this Christmas. Christmas with a tree to decorate, meals to make, friends to celebrate with. Christmas with a loving and patient husband. I vowed to keep my mind from roaming beyond that. To stay present to all that is good.

The terrible sadness is that my dog, Luke, died this past week.

Throughout his thirteen and a half years, Luke, a white Labrador retriever, was my guide to what a life of unflagging optimism and hope can look like.

When I got divorced for the second time and lost all my financial resources to my ex-husband and to the lingering effects of the economic crash of 2008/2009, Luke and I moved from a big house with a pool near Miami to a tiny apartment farther north in the Florida suburbs. I wallowed in shame and self-pity at this reversal in my fortunes. Meanwhile, Luke apparently forgot about the big house with the pool and discovered an equal if not greater amount of joy in our excursions to the muddy local dog park, followed by the exciting hosing off in the dog park "shower."

Throughout his life, Luke was enthusiastic about any trip in the car. Back then, it was our weekly drive to Starbucks for a piece of banana bread to share (all I could afford in the financially tough times when he was a puppy). Later, Alan and I would take long road trips with him stretched out comfortably in his L.L. Bean dog sling in the back seat.

When Alan and I first got together nearly ten years ago, Lukey initially tried to "block" Alan from getting in between the two of us. Soon, however, Luke adopted a new attitude of positioning himself at all times equidistant from Alan and me. He stretched out on top of us on the couch as we watched TV, and at night, he hogged most of our bed from his position in the middle. When Alan and I were married in 2018 in our backyard, Luke, of his own accord, joined my mother in walking me down the aisle; later, as the officiant led Alan and me through our marriage vows, Luke lay down at our feet. Afterward, he wandered around among our guests, accepting appetizers.

He was scared of lightning and always looked at me with concern following the winter explosions from the avalanche guns that we could hear coming from the ski resort—as if he wanted to be sure: *We're not worried about that, are we?* Our neighbors were all potentially interesting to Luke, and more than once, I received a call letting me know that he had wandered down the road and into someone else's house. Though he generally avoided small dogs, Luke showed great patience with cats and allowed my mother's aging and senile feline to literally walk all over him.

Luke survived two health emergencies. The first in 2019, when he likely would have died if we had not found a surgeon bold enough to attempt and successfully execute the removal of a five-pound lipoma from his neck and throat.

The second time, Luke mysteriously collapsed while we were in Maine. The vet had told us Luke would not make it through the next twenty-four hours. And so, we lifted him onto our bed to be close to us, and all night, Luke looked at me, and I looked at him. Once in a while, he would close his eyes, but then open them again and gaze at me. I loved that dog more than I have loved nearly any other living creature in my life. The next morning, Luke was still shaky but back on his feet.

But two years have passed since the last emergency, and in the past six months, Luke has needed to be in a harness most days, so we could hoist him to his feet, down the stairs, or up into the car. Always accommodating and good-natured, Luke even "helped" (with his nose) to put the harness on. He'd been short of breath at times, and our local vet surmised he might have a tumor growing near his heart. We declined when the vet proposed another surgery.

Two days ago, Luke had had a good day. He'd eaten breakfast, shuffled around in the snow in his harness, napped, and finished his dinner. At night, he'd curled up in his bed in our bedroom downstairs where Alan—having contracted COVID—was sleeping while I slept upstairs.

At three o'clock in the morning, Alan woke me up. Luke was having trouble breathing. We carried him to the living room in his bed, and I lay down beside him. He was struggling for air, his neck extended, and in too much distress to be aware of me, I think. I had accepted we were not going to jump in the car and drive the two hours to a twenty-four-hour veterinary hospital in Denver. I think I understood this was Luke's time to pass on, and that what he needed was to be home with us, with me there beside him. After about thirty minutes, his breathing relaxed, and he curled into his bed. I fell asleep, and he was quiet, still. When I awoke in the morning, Luke was no longer alive.

I sobbed when Alan helped me put Luke's body into the car and during the drive to the vet in town to arrange to have Luke's body cremated. Alan and I cried when I returned without Luke to a home where I would never again be greeted by Luke's happy "woo woo *woo!*" made with his head thrown back and a little hop up off his front feet.

Because I am so aware of the lingering, seemingly bottomless sorrow I have felt at other losses, today, what is strange to me is that the most prominent feeling I have toward Luke is of being enormously blessed to have had this great soul in my life. I am profoundly grateful that I was able to give him a good life and that, when it was his time to go, he was surrounded by his human family, and he passed quickly. As one friend told me, "Luke died a prince's death." He was a dog, but he deserved nothing less.

I feel him nearby. And I can say with near certainty that when my time comes to move on from this life, Luke will be there, and I will be following that wagging tail and the excited "woo woo woo" toward whatever is next for the two of us.

The only response I can think of today to your poem:

100 percent I would be me.
Ten out of ten I would live this life again.
And I would find love and joy
Beside my dog, Luke, my best boy.

Love,
Chris

December 16, 2022
New York, New York

O H, CHRIS, SO MUCH LOSS. Your parents, of course, and then
Luke, your companion through some of the darkest and then
most wonderful times of your life. Your love for him and appreciation
of the life lessons he unconsciously embodied is heartbreakingly palpable. What do our losses do to who we are? I'm thinking of my dad, my
battle-axe of a mother-in-law. And most of all, my beloved son.

I had no conflicts with my father, ever. In fairness, he was almost
impossibly cheerful and accommodating to most people and univer-
sally beloved by colleagues, co-workers, friends, and family. Late in
their lives, as my parents transitioned into the constant companionship of retirement, following lives that had long been punctuated by
work, kids, hobbies, and so forth, the closeness could grate. Still, I
can't recall more than a handful of occasions when I heard them raise
their voices to each other. In retrospect, the tension was probably
also provoked by the sudden onslaught of children, grandchildren,
competing schedules, and related demands. But Dad was a steady,
smiling, loving presence, curious to learn, eager to listen, short on
self-aggrandizement—a human version of Luke, a man content. He
is not a cipher to me, even though I miss him.

Dad died two years to the day after my son Yannis's friend Solon,
who was killed by a hit-and-run driver just days short of his fifteenth
birthday. I was with my mother and my brothers and sister at Dad's

bedside; one of my first thoughts on that bleak December day was that Dad would now be there to take care of Solon.

My mother-in-law was never a warm and fuzzy presence in my life, although I grew to have a grudging, exasperated affection for her. In the early years of my marriage, she would dole out measured praise, but what she gave with one hand, she took with the other. My father-in-law died in 1994, a week before my son Yannis (his namesake) was born, so the woman I came to know was thrust into a world where she lived alone, in her midseventies, for the first time since the day she was born. She was unapologetically self-centered and had the tact of a bull in a china shop, but her prejudices were so baldly expressed and so hilariously peculiar that it was hard to take them personally.

She was forthright in declaring that "gardens are for English people because they don't have friends" and that only the vulgar use vinegar instead of lemon on salad (thus condemning the entire nation of France). She also informed me that I did not make brownies correctly, as true American brownies had to have walnuts, since that's how they were served at the American embassy where she worked. She was generally acknowledged to be a terrible cook—in the thirty years that I knew her, I only once ate some tiny spanakopita that were tasty. Her tooth-breaking biscuits were fit only for chucking at stray cats, and her capacity for reducing the Easter *tsoureki* to charcoal was family legend. Nevertheless, she would enquire assiduously about the recipe for any meal she ate at my house and almost invariably concluded that I made it wrong, saying, "Here in Greece, we don't make lasagna with ricotta cheese, only *anthotyro*, with béchamel on top."

As she aged, though, I tried to treat her with humor and kindness, and finally made one dessert (chocolate chip cheesecake) that she adored, and she became more generous with praise. I came to see that I had met her as an old lady who had been raised by a domineering mother and endured a forty-five-year marriage with a bully, and that some of her prickliness was the hedgehog's defense of the soft and squishy bits she had felt the need to protect. My sister-in-law's stories of a laughing, generous, adventurous mother painted a picture of the person she had been before she had been squeezed into a corner many years earlier. I felt compassion for the person who had had her spontaneity and joy drained from her.

But my boy, my Gregos (he preferred "Greg" as he grew, but his childhood nickname, a caress of affection, still comes to me), will always remain a cipher. We shared so much, and I thought I knew him better than anyone else. I still believe that, but it became clear, as his brother and I sifted through the clues hidden in his computer, there was a core of him that he kept inviolate and shared with no one. This core was darkly empowering for him, and I don't know whether he drew strength or comfort from knowing that he had a terrible, implacable, unforgiving choice that he could make when he should so choose.

As a child diagnosed with autism, debilitating food allergies, hearing problems, and a cornucopia of shifting developmental delays, Gregos was the subject of hundreds of hours of interventions from the age of nineteen months until he started college at nineteen years. He was taught, methodically and explicitly, how to walk, speak, use the toilet, and interact with peers. Academic learning was also laborious—specialized tutoring to compensate for central auditory processing disorder, to improve his reading comprehension and spelling. His handwriting remained atrocious, and his math skills were never more than hilariously hit or miss— he could not grasp sizes and proportions of numbers and nearly drove one tutor to distraction as she tried, and failed, to get him to comprehend the rules of geometry. He was physically strong, with a naturally beautiful physique, but had no interest whatsoever in any form of exercise. His brother could persuade him to join brief bouts of one-on-one basketball, but he did not see the point of competitive sports. When he was seven or eight, I had enrolled him in a youth soccer league, and he gave up the ball to his opponent without a murmur. When I asked him why he didn't defend his possession of the ball, he explained to me, as though it was blindingly obvious and I was a bit dense, that the other boy wanted the ball much more than he did. He was a sort of human Ferdinand the Bull, content to smell the flowers and be left alone.

I was so proud of who he had become, the thoughtful, original, sly, and stubborn mind he had developed. He saw connections nobody else saw—it seems he heard music nobody else heard too. He drew strength from his differentness. For his twenty-second birthday, the two of us had taken a weekend car trip to Meteora, the otherworldly medieval monasteries perched on vertiginous stone outcroppings in central Greece. On the long car ride on our way home, he told me that he would not have chosen a life without autism since that was what made his mind unique. I can't help but wonder if he also felt that this gift was a curse since it made it so hard for him to understand the minds of others, but that he kept that feeling hidden. At the time, he seemed so sure.

After he died, soaring and landing, all I could think was that he was my Icarus and that, by attempting to give him wings, I had given him the instrument of his destruction. I am haunted by the story I will never know, as he did not confide in anyone else. I think of how he was drawn to peaks and cliffs, mountain vistas and broad, deep horizons, far more than to the seashore, which is my comfort. At least he knew that I understood that affinity, even if I didn't know the extent of it.

I sometimes wonder if knowing more would help me continue the narrative of our lives. Then I think of his last written words to us, where he declared that his reasons were to remain unknowable, and I am struck with the futility of wanting to know. I could not have loved him more, or less.

> We live with loss as the price of love.
> Take care,
> J

December 20, 2022
Breckenridge, Colorado

I T's NEARLY CHRISTMAS AS I read your latest correspondence and ponder the effects that those we've loved and who are now gone have had upon us. Who we are is tied to who they were; our lives contain their lives. And many of the questions they've left us with will now never be answered. How do we make sense of all the unknowns?

I never really got over my childhood Christmases—the giddy excitement as the Christmas tablecloth and holiday decorations appeared, the presents wrapped in secret, and the smell of cardamom from *bulla*, the baked loaves of Swedish Christmas bread. There were exciting trips to New York City to see *The Nutcracker* ballet at Lincoln Center and ice skate beneath the towering Christmas tree in front of Rockefeller Plaza.

My father's parents, who possessed impeccable Mayflower and New York Social Register pedigrees, had died in a car crash when I was seven. And so, my mother's immigrant parents took prominence in our family. These proud Scandinavian grandparents—my grandfather a successful, status-conscious entrepreneur, my grandmother easily mistaken for Ingrid Bergman—ensured that Christmas Eve at their colonial home above the Hudson River was a glamorous event, a champagne and caviar cocktail party followed by a formal dinner. Their tree, the decorations, the table—everything was adorned in red, gold, and the flickering lights of the Nordic season of *Jul*.

Most of these family members are gone now. And yet I still see us all so clearly, wearing our fanciest clothes—cocktail or formal dress—the women in heels with curled or upswept hair. From the rustling fabrics worn by my mother, grandmother, and aunt wafted the seductively adult scents of Chanel or Jean Patou. Those Christmas evenings were not meant to impress others but to recognize—to revel in—something we believed about ourselves as a family.

We were a family of beautiful women. Everyone said so. And there must have been some truth to it, for I remember noticing, as a child, how heads turned in the dining room of the New York Athletic Club on Central Park South at Christmastime as the maître d' ushered us to our reserved table for dinner. I soaked in the admiring looks, as I am sure the adults in my family did too.

A portrait of my grandmother in an off-the-shoulder evening gown gazed at us from over the fireplace in my grandparents' living room. According to family legend, the artist, an Austrian count, had begged her to allow the watercolor sketch because he was so captivated by her beauty.

My grandparents were proud when, at the age of twenty and the height of her youthful allure to men, my mother had dazzled my father on the New England ski slopes and made a most successful marriage with this New York lawyer, a graduate of both Princeton and Yale. Similarly, they took great pleasure in the remarkable beauty of her younger sister, my aunt, who, through most of her life, wielded the superpower of magically obtaining from men (and sometimes even women) whatever she wanted.

In my immediate family, my elven-faced sister, as a teenager, exploded into Debbie Harry, Studio 54 glamor. I, on the other hand, always teetered on the edge of "pretty." Often a few pounds too heavy, I endured seemingly endless years of braces and acne. "But you are very good at school, sweetheart," my parents remarked with an off-hand tone that humiliated me.

I lost weight, began to wear makeup, and hung on as best I could to my membership in the club of beautiful women. This fixation on an attractive physical appearance came with the dark companions of insecurity, resentment, and sometimes cruelty.

My grandmother was born in Sweden to a beautiful, high-spirited society mother who had no intention of marrying her Russian lover—my grandmother's father. As a child, little Margareta became a social embarrassment and was sent to school in England. She must have understood both that she was unwanted and that it was vitally important for her to do her best to be pleasing to adults and, later, attractive and desirable to men. She experienced rejection by a fiancé when he discovered she was "a bastard." She passed this story and the parting gift the man gave her—a lovely brooch—on to my mother. A warning? My mother passed the story and the brooch on to me.

Margareta eventually married Carl-Eric, a salesman at a Finnish paper company where she worked as a multilingual secretary. Together, the young married couple traveled across the Atlantic on a minesweeper in the late 1930s from Europe. In America, Margareta and Carl-Eric quickly advanced up the social and economic ladder. Years later, as the matriarch of the family, my grandmother became the model of self-centeredness, but also—well into her nineties—incredibly charming and irresistible as a conversationalist to men of all ages. She still spoke several languages too. I remember how flattered I felt when she showed interest in me, declaring when I returned from a college semester in France that she and I must now speak "only French" together.

She and my grandfather could be harsh if they believed the actions of any one of us tarnished the reputation of the family. During my first marriage to a man they despised, they persuaded all my family to refuse to speak to me. The ban was lifted after I finally divorced this husband.

My grandmother had the mixed blessing of living to 104. Even at that age, my aunt and my mother still spoke about her beauty: her thick hair, her smooth skin. When I visited her in the nursing home a year before she died, with the man I am married to now, Alan, like a rival, she informed me—while looking at him—"I could have him, you know."

My mother and I were best friends throughout most of my childhood. But as the "one who did well in school," I wanted to go to college. Later, I moved to New York City, and longed to travel, explore, and take chances. As a young adult, the last thing I dreamt of was a life like my mother's, and she knew it. How must this have made her feel? Hurt, betrayed, perhaps scared for me? She imagined a comfortable life for me, a life like hers with a good man like my father. What would happen to me if I made different choices?

When we were all much younger, my mother's relationship with her sister had been filled with laughter and teasing competitiveness but fraught just below the surface. Later, my mother rarely missed an opportunity to point out how my grandparents had spoiled and pampered my aunt in preparation for the glorious and successful match they assumed their most exquisite daughter would make—but never quite did.

After my grandparents' deaths, the two sisters, now in their seventies, battled over my grandparents' country house, which neither could afford to keep. While their joint inheritance dwindled, my aunt fought to hold on to this property that perhaps reminded her of a time when she—when all of us—believed that life held only admiration, good fortune, and success.

In the months before my mother's death from cancer, my aunt behaved with a cruelty toward my frail, weakened mother that shocked me and my siblings, and the decision was made to block my aunt's relentless accusatory texts, emails, and phone messages to my mother. In the end, it was my mother who made the choice not to speak to her sister before she died.

And of my sister and me? In my younger sister, the family beauty appeared as another brilliant comet. But as we've grown older, and looks have faded, her unpredictable temper has often left her isolated, with more time to spend online engaging in angry political exchanges.

For my part, the surgery on my brain has caused me to lose the ability to truly judge how I look. Perhaps that is not a bad thing. Whatever girlish beauty once graced those of us who remain is long gone, or it might be kinder to say that whatever beauty we still possess is of the inward sort.

As Christmas approaches, I drag in a pine tree from the woods behind our house in Breckenridge and decorate it with white lights, a thick red-and-gold ribbon that curves through the branches from top to bottom, and the few remaining ornaments from my childhood. Memories spark of the elegant family parties of half a century ago: a tree aglow with lights and bedecked with traditional red and gold Scandinavian ornaments, a sturdy straw goat wrapped in red ribbon—the Christmas *Julbock*—on the mantle. My grandfather handing me a glass of champagne, nodding with an approving smile at the young woman he thinks he sees when he looks at me. I find myself adrift in that fantasy I have entertained for almost all of my life. It will pain me when I shake it off, but I cannot stop myself from entering and lingering for a while in this version of my past:

> Once upon a time, there was a storybook family of beautiful women. We knew no uncertainty or fear, and our futures, rarely considered, were secure. Each one of us in some measure, girl or woman, shared the gift of grace and loveliness. We were princesses in a fairy tale with kingdoms spread out before us.

> Wherever you are in the world, my dear friend,
> Merry Christmas and a Happy New Year,
> Chris

December 29, 2022
New York, New York

YOUR DESCRIPTION OF CHRISTMASES PAST evoked so many images and memories for me. My childhood Christmases were magical, from the ritual of choosing and cutting our own Christmas tree to the loving placement of ornaments acquired over our lifetimes. The crèche that my father built from a scavenged wine box and packing straw and twigs he and my mother gathered in Central Park, the traditional carols, scents of ginger, nutmeg, and cinnamon. I remember counting down the days in college before we could all be reunited and enveloped by the ineffable sense of love and security that Christmas was always the same.

After I had children of my own, I tried to recreate that feeling for them, making the same Christmas cookies that my mother had made, continuing the tradition of adding a new ornament per child to the tree every year, exclaiming over the handmade decorations that benchmarked the progress of clumsy childish hands. I loved the annual resurrection of memories, traditions, hymns, and carols, hearing my father sing "O Holy Night" at midnight Mass. Since Greg died, I cannot face any of it. I brought our ornaments with me from Greece, but they're stored in boxes at my mother's house.

For this year, it was a blessed relief to be free of the visual trappings of the western Christmas and to travel with a friend and my son Yannis to Rio. The hot, humid, almost liquid air, the astonishing fecundity of the tropical jungles carpeting the steep hills encircling Rio de Janeiro in jaw-dropping contrast to the sugary-sand beaches and clear turquoise waters, all of it was foreign and exotic enough to let me forget that this was the holiday I had always celebrated with great joy and anticipation.

This was my third Christmas in the "after" times, each of them very different from the other and markedly different from "before." Rio was the most disconnected, the heat and summer clothing making it feel utterly new and different. I didn't need to work to forget and could just enjoy the novelty of the place for a few days—all this courtesy of a dear friend of the heart I've known since September 1983, when we were both cowed first-year law students. In the intervening years, he's known hard-earned professional success and recognition. He has also suffered indelible personal losses, and I think that's affected how he treats people. He can be prickly, but he is also brilliant, generous, and the kindest man I know.

But memory sneaks in, doesn't it? Yannis and I made the obligatory tourist trek to the peak of Corcovado, standing below the eighty-meter statue of Christ the Redeemer, gazing out at the lush landscape below; each of us, privately, thinking how much Greg would have loved the soaring sensation of viewing things from above. And immediately thereafter, reflecting on the fact that, if he were alive, we would still be living in the before times and would most likely not be here at all.

Later in the week, sitting in the rooftop bar of a lovely hotel overlooking Ipanema, talking about food and experiences and things we missed, I mentioned the singular meteorological phenomenon of late January in Greece, the "halcyon days," where there is almost always a week or ten days of mild temperatures and full sun. What feels like the entire population of Athens descends on the Attic seacoast on those Sundays, sitting outdoors in down vests like grateful basilisks, soaking up the gentle sunlight together with ouzo and seafood mezes like grilled octopus, calamari, and *marides*; it seems to give everyone just enough reprieve from the winter and a taste of hope for the spring to come, all wrapped in the communal sense of gratitude and common experience.

I must have sounded wistful because my friend turned to me and gave me a hug, saying, "It's okay, you just miss Greece!" But I knew it wasn't Greece I missed. I missed the feeling of a time when life felt like a childhood Christmas, when it was somehow more pure, less complicated, full of hope and simple satisfactions. In those days, I loved and trusted my husband. I loved the place where I was living, despite the traffic and the chaos. My children were small, all the frustrations were temporary, and the hurts and missteps were small and remediable.

The thin membrane that constitutes the mental separation from the before times buckled and burst, casting the memories of before and after into an untidy eddy of sorrow, grief, gratitude, and wonder for the way life sneaks up on you and changes utterly overnight.

And yet, even in the after times, there is so much to be grateful for, so much to see and smile at. Yannis, so bruised and damaged by loss and hurt, yet actively pursuing his own healing and resolution, is a source of both pride and inspiration. Good friends who don't shy away from the complicated mess of feelings, who acknowledge that their experience, too, contains joy and pain and reflection and optimism and that the whole thing is a bit of a mess, but that's what it is. My sister's holiday photo, with Mom and the rest of her clan, grinning on a frigid North Carolina mountaintop.

What will ensue in the coming year? I wonder. Will I find a place to work that brings a level of fulfillment, purpose? Will I plant my butt in a chair long enough to write the hard things in a way that will illuminate not only my own thinking but also provide some light for other questing souls? Will I meet someone who makes me think that maybe I should be open to the possibility of a new partner?

For now, I will head out into the cold, bright midday light of late December in New York, smile at the waterfowl congregating on the reservoir and the glow on the faces of the children seeing the city for the first time, and I will try to open my heart to the possibilities of after.

Hoping the New Year will bring light and
purpose to our lives,
Jane

January 2, 2023
Breckenridge, Colorado

I HAVE HAD A VERY hard time responding to your lovely, hopeful letter. When I sit down to write, all my thoughts are angry and fearful, all the memories I try to summon overwhelm me with pain.

Twenty twenty-two was the year I was diagnosed with a brain tumor.

In the months before that devastating March MRI, I was in the home stretch of finishing my first novel. I was part of an active writers' group, and at our local community center, a dozen local writers had asked me to lead a second writing workshop. These workshops, in particular, led me to believe that I had finally found a place in sports-oriented Summit County, Colorado, where I have always felt like an outsider. Alan and I were discovering more and more enjoyment in the weekend cottage we'd bought a year before, two hours west in Colorado's picturesque, high-desert wine country.

I was still struggling with grief over the death of my mother in 2019 and my father in 2013. I missed them terribly, missed their stories and seeing the world through their eyes. And with these deaths, too, came the loss of the person I was who only existed in the complicated but deeply meaningful relationships I had with each of my parents. I mourned as family traditions were abandoned and as the close relationships I'd had with my sister and my aunt disintegrated.

But, in this *before time*, I was also coming to believe that maybe I was reaching some kind of understanding with grief and loss, that I was working my way, with some measure of growth, into the "Elder" stage of life. Becoming older and wiser.

Then, I had brain surgery in April 2022.

Today, the daily radiation treatments at the hospital following surgery, which required Alan and me to move temporarily to Denver, are six months in the past. This month marks my final, exhausting cycle of oral chemo. I'll continue with a study drug and MRI scans every two months. I try to live each day with hope and purpose, but the thought of death is always there: It waits for me each morning; I escape from it by retreating to bed early at night.

There are things I can do—a yoga practice, a walk in the woods, calling a friend—that help me disengage for a little while from the sense of anger and existential dread. The fact that this correspondence with you has made me want to write again represents a huge U-turn away from the destination of complete despair I was headed toward. Now, let me pull my head out of the storm cloud of self-pity that follows me around. Because there are some important gifts in this *time after* that I want to name:

Home after surgery, I lay in bed awake for hours, watching the moon drift in its arching path over the snow-covered mountains. Time slowed. I felt the presence of God and that I was not alone.

In the period of recovery, I celebrated Passover with Alan's family, and it seemed to me the shadow of death had literally passed over me.

Alan has MS, and I always expected that I would one day be the caretaker. How humbling it is to accept his caretaking, how astonishing to open my eyes and see, fully, how endlessly loving and patient he is. I hear strength and tenderness in his voice. I never expected to have this kind of love in my life.

One day, one of us—Alan or I—will be left without the other, and I expect it will be him. I know now that I could not bear to be the one of us left without the other. He has taken on that burden.

I am overwhelmed by the love of friends and family, and of neighbors in our community. All these months later, I still receive cards, emails, and texts from people who are just checking in to see how I am doing. And though it is corny, I love it when my neighbors say, "You look great! You are such an inspiration!" I mean, what else are they going to say? But somehow, it makes me feel that I am actually doing something positive for the neighborhood, just by getting out there and taking a walk.

A local independent publisher took on my novel and, with the help of a group of freelance publishing friends, got it out into the world in record time, allowing me the joy and satisfaction of holding a copy in my hands.

I am still in seemingly good health with good energy. I exercise; I have an appetite.

Though I was not able to travel back in time to relive the Thanksgivings or Christmases of my childhood, I was able to be self-aware enough to stand in Whole Foods before the holidays and feel an unexpected rush of gratitude that I was not alone, that I had people I care about *here and now* to spend the holidays with, a shopping list of things to buy so that I could contribute and be a part of something.

I understand that we will all die and that not everyone gets time in which to process this, to focus on what matters, to perhaps reach some sort of deeper understanding of life. But why did this moment have to show up now when I still feel so young? Too young. In Yann Martel's *The Life of Pi*, the narrator cries out to the universe with a terrible and familiar anguish: "I am lost at sea, alone, in a boat with a tiger!" What is my tiger? What if I were to approach this tiger, speak to it? I try to see that it is a gift to be given more time to ask these questions and perhaps find some answers.

Even in this strange, extreme state of knowing I have an illness that will kill me, I observe my ridiculous, achievement-oriented need to "do this" (whatever "this" is) successfully. I feel driven to discover the Ultimate Meaning of Life and Death, as I explained last week in my twice-monthly call with Jake, the oncology social worker at the hospital. And I was grateful to be able to laugh at myself and let go of a sense of burden and my own self-importance when he pointed out with the wise-ass, East Coast humor we share: "Sister, no one is expecting you to crack the code of existence."

Like you, holding on to the hope of a New Year
filled with good things,
Chris

January 4, 2023
New York, New York

T HE EXPERIENCE OF THE CRUELTY of mortality so aptly lends itself to the muscular image of a gorgeous predator. How is that? Being faced with the uncrackable code of existence evokes all the emotions I can imagine would arise from being forced to share a small, inescapable space with a dangerous yet seductive beast. There's a cool, tantalizing beauty that whispers and beckons, a sense that you are an initiate into a realm that few have experienced, that you are now blooded with knowledge that is terrible and great. The wonder is matched by terror, as that knowledge is as pitiless and implacable as it is stark and weirdly elegant. You circle it warily, knowing that it can kill you, that it will kill you one day, but in the meantime, there is something entrancing, even empowering, about being able to stare into its eyes and not be blinded. You have acquired a superpower, an ability to feel love and wonder and gratitude with a synaesthetic intensity. Experiences that would once have been felt lightly and immediately forgotten assume a sweetness, a beauty that you can savor and roll on your tongue and across your heart, as velvety and luscious as the first sip of a good cabernet. But the cost is—the cost is everything. And you had no choice in the matter. And the universe's indifferent imposition of this tiger on you, with all the intensity of emotion that you now experience, the joy and the anger and the tenderness and the rage of impotence, feels unimaginably cruel.

But here you are. The boat sails through beautiful waters, through music and taste and moonlight and embraces, the brush of your husband's hand across your palm as you walk together into the medical center or turn homeward after a walk in the weak but hopeful afternoon sun of a January sky. Can you embrace the journey for its richness? Can you accept the extraordinary gift of surrendering to another's devotion, even though it was a gift you never wanted? Can you marvel at the supple, sinuous beauty of the tiger's coat? You can be on guard for the twitch of its tail and still marvel at its capacity for stillness; there are even moments when you can forget the threat that it embodies—perhaps.

I spent a long walk today nattering around Central Park, listening to a podcast on election politics and the circular firing squad that is the Republican caucus in the House of Representatives, then another British podcast on the enduring power of Demosthenes's Philippics, his perorations on the dangers of the Macedonians under Philip. How pointless and marvelous it is that we have studied his peerless command of rhetoric and persuasive argument for nearly 2,400 years, and even more gloriously pointless that we know his contemporaries sniped at his defense of Athenian purity by insinuating that his mother had Scythian blood. People have changed so little.

I stopped on a bench to watch a unique New York tableau—a Black man, early sixties, I judged, was fishing from the western bank of the lake, sufficiently unusual to capture my curiosity. His light rod, bent, seemed in danger of snagging on shoreline branches and muck. Still, he reeled it in, patiently and (to my ignorant eyes) skillfully, placing his net within reach and finally slipping a foot-long fish into the net and onto the pavement. His movements were practiced, spare and efficient. He unhooked the fish gently, took a photo with his phone after wiping the fish slime off his hands. Another admirer offered to take his photo, so he handed off his phone to pose with said fish, shifting position obediently at the urgings of his temporary social media manager. He then stepped back over the low railing and hurled the fish back into the water, splashing and startling the two young women sitting on the boat landing who, intent on their phones, had missed the entire catch-and-release drama. I then watched him extract a can of Jolly Green Giant corn niblets from his bag and bait his hook once more.

I got up and moved on, focusing again on the tale of Demosthenes, who, as it turns out, took his own life rather than face punishment at the hands of Philip's Macedonians once they finally did overthrow the greatly weakened Athenian state. This was considered an honorable end, and he was regarded as wise for having chosen death rather than allowing humiliation and possibly a torturous death at the hands of his enemies. Inevitably, I compared his choice to my Greg's, and the complicated feelings I have about the courage it took for him to do what he did.

All of this jumbled together in my day, the particular with the universal, the amusing and human with the eternal and tragic, the sheer magnificence of human trust and emotion, the inescapable fact that things end. I catch glimpses of my tiger at the oddest moments.

Much love,
Jane

January 9, 2023
Breckenridge, Colorado

I WILL CONFRONT MY TIGER with questions, even though I fear what the answers may be.

The creature crouches at the stern of the boat, wrapped in its shimmering coat of shadows and destruction. Pinned beneath a blanket of nightmares, I cannot move from my corner at the bow. It's just us two, adrift in the vast and borderless ocean.

My voice shakes as I try to master my fear. "Tell me your name."

It chuckles and swings its big head into view, smiling sharp teeth. "Why should I, orphan girl? What do I care about you and your meaningless life?"

"Why do you call me that?"

"Do you really need me to tell you, *orphan girl?* You did not belong in the family that raised you. They rejected you. You know they did. Their choices were so sensible and led to such smooth outcomes. To houses and children, and now grandchildren." It curves a long, black-and-orange striped tail around its feet comfortably. "To lives filled with the lovely things that come to lovely people. While *you . . .*" The creature sneers. "Need I say more?"

I want to belong to my family; these words land like a blow. But who is speaking, is it the tiger? *Is it me?* "Who are you? What is your name?"

The moon dips and shines through the clouds. The creature withdraws in silence to its corner.

"Musicians," I whisper as an idea slides into my mind on a

moonbeam. "And artists. Writers." My voice becomes louder, "And there were adventurers, too, in my father's family—one came across the ocean to find a new land. One climbed the Andes to take the first photographs of Machu Picchu. Another left a high society life to start a sheep ranch in Australia. And one," I smile with satisfaction, "well, she married the grandson of a pirate!"

The creature sneers. "Who do you think you are? Someone special? It was your responsibility in the family story to marry well, stand behind your husband, have children, and live in a large, spotless house. Don't tell me you didn't understand the importance of having the right politics, of praying to the correct God. Those are the real stories that came to matter, to define your family. If you hadn't been so self-centered, you might have understood. If you'd played your part correctly, you would have belonged."

Its voice drones on, but I am not listening. Instead, I am asking myself, what if I was not an orphan who led a meaningless life? What if that is just a particular spin, like "fake news?" Or, maybe the genetic concoction that came together as "me" was stirred up from some earlier part of the family lore, chapters that were forgotten or no longer seemed relevant to some? But they matter to me. To me, they are part of our story too.

Like me, those members of my family in these forgotten pages would have been mesmerized by the swallows careening through the vast space beneath the Peruvian Andes, by the great snow-capped *Apus* rising up and ringing 'round the Sacred Valley, by the lonely Pyramid of the Magician still humming with ancient power in the forests of the Yucatan; or by the silent mystery of petroglyphs reached only by ladder above the Colorado River, cliff carvings that still communicate to us over thousands of years.

These great- great- greatgrandfathers and mothers (and great aunts or uncles) would have been drawn to the spectacle of ships from every corner of the world jostling into Hong Kong harbor, as ships have done for centuries, to the busy piazzas in the ancient Italian city of star-crossed lovers, known also for Dante, and for tyrants with names like Big Dog. They had seen so much; they wouldn't have been surprised that in this one city, Pisanello's plump quail nestled beside an angelic blonde Madonna in a tiny chapel while outside, suspicious citizens spread gossip about their neighbors in secret notes stuffed through mouths carved into the stone walls around the piazza.

Like me, these distant relatives might have wanted to gather a handful of acorns at the Temple of Apollo from oak trees that trace their lineage back as far as the fifth century BC temple, or they might have lain sprawled in the grass like druids on midsummer in northern Scotland while the unsetting sun resisted the pull of night above Arthur's Seat.

And surely, they would have raised a glass to love.

I stare down the creature with whom I share this boat. "I know your name now, and it is *Liar*. It is the *Teller of False Tales*. One day, I will die, but I will not die from regret that I did not set out beyond the borders of safety to see the world, to try to learn something I could not learn at home, to find love after so many failures.

"You cannot frighten me by making me feel I am no one. I am a child of my family, not an orphan. Even if I do come from the part that was buried or forgotten. I remember. Those eccentric relatives and their stories matter to me. I belong to my family too."

As our boat bumps the shore and the sun rises, the creature glances at me over its shoulder and then leaps overboard. And as if that tiger had been a part of me, I feel lighter now as the animal disappears without a backward glance. Leaving only pawprints on the sandy beach.

Chris

January 16, 2023
New York, New York

Y OU'VE FOUND A CONNECTION TO the heroes in your family history as a means to confront your tiger, and I'm smiling at the
strength it has given you. As I wander around the city, grasping at the
moments when it feels like home, I turn for guidance and solace to
my maternal grandmother. She lived until I was in my midtwenties
and out of law school, a frail, vibrant, unceasingly optimistic presence. She had suffered heart attacks and a stroke that left her with
aphasia and had endured the indignity of a colostomy bag with grace
and humor for nearly the last thirty years of her life, but never talked
about her aches and pains. "Oh, I'm fine," she'd say. "Tell me what
you're doing!"

Unlike you, I do not have Mayflower genes—three of my grandparents were Irish immigrants, and my paternal grandmother
was the daughter of Irish immigrants. (And those immigrants
were bootleggers, but that's another story.) My parents were the
first generation to go to college, and my father's admission to Yale
College was vetoed by the priest who told my grandparents that he
would lose his faith if he attended that Protestant institution. (His
admission and full scholarship had been engineered by the members of the New York Yale Club who were fond of my grandfather,
the chief bartender, and who knew Mike had a smart kid.) Dad went
to Fordham, where he could commute, live at home, and save both
money and his Catholic soul.

I try now to imagine my grandmother Johanna, known as Josie. To me, she was always an old lady. When I look now at the few photos of her as a young woman, seen through the prism of my sixty-one-year-old eyes, I can catch a glimpse of who she was. My mother, her daughter, who at a vigorous eighty-five has outlived her mother's lifespan, colors the black-and-white images with stories and recollections.

Age seventeen, tall, cornflower-blue, slightly nearsighted eyes, dark red hair to her waist, carefully plaited and coiled to look as neat and presentable as possible to the officials in New York harbor, which was fast approaching. She had a photo of her Uncle Jim, her grandmother's brother, who looked like all the lanky, narrow-faced Russell men she'd known growing up, their irrepressible sense of humor evident in the lines around the mouth. Her heart must have been pounding with fear and excitement—what if he wasn't there to meet her? How could she ever navigate the vast city beyond the enormous harbor?

It had been her parents' decision, and she had had little say in the matter—she was to make money and send it home so her parents could keep up the payments on the farm and take care of the four younger brothers and sisters. She was bright and a good student, and her Aunt Ellie had pleaded with her parents to let her study, offering to pay the tuition at the convent high school in Thurles. "Josie's so smart; all the nuns say it's a pity to pull her out of school; she could become a teacher!" But money was tight, and the income from a distant teaching job was too inconsequential. Not to mention the fact that teachers were old maids, and Josie was bold, curious, quick to laugh, but sometimes hot-tempered. I'm sure the prospect of life as a spinster, beating grammar and composition into young heads, was not especially appealing. So, she chose to see it as an adventure and ignore the stinging hurt of being sent away.

The months of correspondence with the New York cousins had offered an attractive option—the combination of her good looks, grammatical English, and experience with younger siblings made Josie an ideal nanny. This was a desirable, genteel job that would not be physically strenuous. The New York families who could afford a nanny paid well, and as it happened, one of Uncle Jim's colleagues had a friend whose daughter could put in a good word for her.

I try to imagine how Manhattan must have seemed to a country girl whose sole experience of urban life had been occasional trips to the market town of Thurles and the brief glimpse of Cork City, where the houses were in rows tight upon each other. She lived with her cousins on East 97th Street, one brownstone in the endless stretch of brownstones, all cheek by jowl. Trees were confined to woeful squares in the sidewalk, and everything was paved; only Central Park would have offered a familiar vista of rolling grass, trees, ponds, and flowers. But what excitement, what energy! Everything must have been new, intimidating and eye-opening.

She was lucky from the start. The children in her first family were well-behaved, not so close in age that they would challenge her authority, but close enough to love her humor and enthusiasm about learning new things. The family was fond of her and treated her well. The other household staff, from the cook to the maids and drivers, embraced the unworldly teenager far from her family and schooled her on the unwritten rules.

Josie quickly learned to observe, stay quiet, and not assume any familiarity with the family. And she reveled in all the experiences her rural upbringing could never have prepared her for. She accompanied the children to art lessons, concerts, parks, and parties, taking part in activities that would otherwise be off limits to an immigrant girl from Tipperary with a grammar school education. She discovered the delights of the public library and read voraciously on her days off when she returned to the Russell family in the brownstone on 97th Street.

Seven years passed in the blink of an eye, and suddenly, Josie was a self-assured twenty-five-year-old with money in her pocket even after sending money home. She would have been easily familiar with most of Manhattan, privy to rarified environments. Dressed in stylish hand-me-downs from her employer's daughter, she had met Eleanor Roosevelt at the Rivington Street Settlements, marveled at the vast halls of the Metropolitan Museum, and sat spellbound at the Metropolitan Opera and the Philharmonic. Summers found her tending to skinned knees and sunburns in luxurious cabins in the Adirondacks, where distance and heat relaxed the rules. Mom has a photo of her with a broad smile, a willowy young woman in a swimsuit, her long auburn hair loose.

After the end of one assignment, with the next one lined up after the summer, she was able to make the long sea journey home to see her family on a month-long visit. Seven years of missing them, letting her imagination fill in between the lines of her mother's cramped handwriting. The tissue-paper blue airmail envelopes probably arrived once a month or so, and she would have savored the short letters describing the day-to-day life on the farm, the arrival of two more siblings whose faces she had to imagine.

I wonder what she hoped for as she stood on the prow and sailed into Cobh harbor. I thought of my experience on my far more frequent trips back to New York from Greece, expecting to slip back in to home like putting on a worn slipper, and ultimately feeling conflicted, at once home and uprooted, comfortable and confined. Were her siblings awed but ironic, too, sly and amused by the subtle changes in her pronunciation, her American words, and her American dress? I recall on summer visits to Amagansett momentarily forgetting the English word for something or responding to one of the boys in Greek and glimpsing my mother's half-amused, half-distressed expression.

And then life moved so fast. Josie returned to New York, married her Johnny, left the glamor of the 5th Avenue families, raised and educated two girls and a boy. All her children went to college and made happy marriages and families—she had nine grandchildren, all born into relative privilege. Her hunger for education was transmitted to her children and their children, some of whom went to the same Ivy League colleges attended by the children of the families she had worked for.

My grandmother was always keenly self-aware, and I wonder if she thought about who her grandchildren saw. The mirror would have shown them a middle-aged, slightly portly lady, in sensible heels and dresses, a sagging chin, her body no longer willowy but squared by age and childbirth. I failed to perceive, despite her curiosity about current events and the goings-on in our lives, her appreciation of jokes and anecdotes, the lithe young woman who had seen so much in such a short period of time, before the conventions of family life and Catholic community expectations limited her to home and the company of other mothers. To me, she was simply Nano, a soft lilt and the occasional old-fashioned word betraying her foreignness, although, in every other aspect, she looked like all the other grandmothers out with their families for Mother's Day lunch. On the many occasions that something would strike her fancy, I remember that her laugh would ring out, young and unrestrained.

I have one strong memory of when I saw the girl she had been. It came to me now as I sit writing in the apartment I have only recently moved into, which is barely a stone's throw from where Nano lived when she first landed in New York. I had returned from a semester in Ireland in 1981 and told her about singing in pubs and eating Halloween brack; her face lit up, and she was transported to a girl of sixteen. She told me the story of how her friends had dared her to walk through the cemetery on Halloween, and, quaking but defiant, she sauntered through, cool and serene, shaking in her bones but determined not to let it show. Today, as I muster the courage to embrace the unknown at the age of sixty-one, I remember her laugh and the bold spirit that animated a girl who began a new life at seventeen and never forgot how to savor it.

Here's to channeling strong women with humor and curiosity,

Love,

J

January 23, 2023
Breckenridge, Colorado

W HAT IF WE CARRY WITHIN us the memory of simple pleasures, of burning ambition, of uncertainty and hope, passed
from lives lived not by immediate family but by others whose paths
we may have crossed? What if this is true, even if we have only trod
the same ground and looked out over the same valley or river as these
others may have done? "For every atom belonging to me," wrote Walt
Whitman in *Leaves of Grass*, "as good belongs to you."

And from those whose genes we carry, how much is passed from
one generation to the next?

Alan and I, seeking a distraction from the cold of Breckenridge and
the ever-present worry about my health, packed up the car and drove
south to Arizona. For a few days, we settled into a lovely small inn on
the west side of Sedona beneath Thunder Mountain.

On day one it snowed, and we read by the fire. The next day, we
explored. Passing through a valley of towering red monoliths and
redolent green juniper and pine, we visited an ancient cliff dwelling. Constructed over one thousand years ago, the many chambers
tucked into the cliff face looked out over a forest of white sycamore, a
bright and turbulent river, and an expanse of valley. There was shade
and cool, clear rushing water, and plants whose roots, seeds, and
bark offered food. Likely plenty of game for hunters. Corn and cotton were grown in the valley too.

Unlike the cliff communities of Mesa Verde in southern Colorado, which had to be accessed by ropes from above and seemed clearly constructed as a kind of defense against enemies or the elements—this cliff community appeared to be the work of individuals who had found a beautiful place where all their needs could be met, including even the aesthetic pleasure of a beautiful and far-ranging view.

Walking along the river beneath the layered cliffs where ladders once connected one level to the next, I could sense the contentment that existed here hundreds of years ago, at least for a time, among the residents. Somewhere deep in my genetic or imaginative past as an American, I held the essential knowledge of what it was like to exist in a kind of natural Eden, surrounded by the safe web of community. And living in complete harmony with one's surroundings, why would anyone ever want to leave?

But the cliff-dwellers did leave. According to the Park Service history, no one knows why (unlike Mesa Verde, where enemies and cannibalism destroyed the communities. I swear, you can still sense that evil hundreds of years later). One theory is that the community was lured by the promise of grand, imagined opportunities to the northeast, passed on by random travelers along the river. Was it simply an itch to their collective imagination that had to be scratched, that became enough for them all to abandon paradise?

On another day in Arizona, we drove up 8,000 feet to visit the old mining town of Jerome—a town not unlike the mining town of Breckenridge, where we now live. Here, the smell of ambition, greed, and destruction hangs in the air, just as the remnants of old buildings hang precariously off the steep sides of the mountain—drafty living quarters, a saloon and a brothel, a church. Overseeing it all, at the very precipitous top of the peak and above the heap of tailings vomited forth from its deep shaft, is the old copper mine itself.

Intrepid nineteenth-century entrepreneurs scoured the West for sites like this with their teams of geologists; investors from the East funded their efforts, and desperate and ambitious men executed the dangerous work, descending narrow mines as deep as the Empire State building is tall. Few of these men got rich; most died in accidents or from illness.

I have a gut feeling for this ambition, so raw and American, and for the obliviousness to the danger that might lead one to join such an effort. I know what it is like to believe that this time, it will be different. This effort will be successful. I can imagine losing everything to one half-baked idea. I can imagine it because I have followed that trail of breadcrumbs.

On our last night in Sedona, as I thought about what gets passed down from one generation of family to the next, I did an internet search for my grandmother. I found an announcement in the *New York Times* from 1928 of invitations going out for the wedding of my father's parents, Elizabeth Bell Otis and John Knight Holbrook. It mentions that Miss Otis was living with her grandmother, the wife of the late Elisha Otis, inventor of the elevator.

Elizabeth was not living with her own mother. Her mother had, I remembered, divorced Charles Otis and begun a new family with John Morgan in California. Passed off to her grandmother on the East Coast, my grandmother was a child without a mother. In this, she was not unlike my mother's mother, who was abandoned by her Swedish mother and Russian father and sent away to boarding school in England. My great-grandmothers gave up what might have been most dear to them in their pursuit of what they believed would make a better life; my grandmothers came of age having to make their own choices and mistakes without the guidance of a mother.

My own mother was handed off to a relative in Finland in 1939 or 1940 and then whisked north to Lapland for the duration of World War II when her parents left Europe for the United States. Because of the war, my grandparents did not return for several years to Finland, by which time my mother's whereabouts were unknown. But my grandfather had become the US salesman for a Finnish company that produced newsprint; with the help of the Hearst family, which purchased enormous quantities of newsprint for their publications and had extensive communication channels all over the world, my grandparents were able to locate my mother.

What do I make of all this, the lines of imaginative and genetic history? To me, it feels distinctly American—an abandoned Eden, a struggle for riches and power, the gaps that children fall through throughout all our history, as parents, grandparents, and great-grandparents grappled with their own choices and desires within a changing society and an often-fragile web of community.

What makes us leave what is beautiful and nurturing to struggle against what is brutal and hard? How do I explain to myself the mothers and grandmothers who left their daughters to the care of others to pursue their own paths? In their youth, motherhood must have seemed a burden, but did they mourn or regret this choice later in life? What scars did this leave? Was my decision not to become a mother my unconscious wish to answer this question?

I add to this piece a short epilogue: our road trip took us from Sedona to California. On our way back home to Breckenridge, we stopped overnight, for timing and convenience, at the casino town of Mesquite, Nevada—an alarming oasis of bright lights and slot machines in the middle of the desert. While the Eureka Hotel was convenient and very cheap, getting dinner required a walk through the busy, clanging casino to get to the restaurant.

Games of luck and chance seem to be a quintessential part of the American experience. They arrived with the earliest settlers from Europe, men and women who aggressively worked to replace the native population. In a great irony, today, many of the most popular casinos are run by Native American tribes.

As we walked through the casino and passed elderly men and women riveted to the flash and noise of slot machines, I thought about a remark an ex-husband of mine had once made. He came from a working-class family, in which his grandmother had loved to gamble. She had been considered by his family to be "lucky," though I don't believe this luck ever changed the family's economic fortunes. My ex believed that he, too, had inherited this quality of luck. As far as I know, no amount of monetary difficulties—before, during, or after our marriage—would convince him otherwise.

Blind optimism or pure self-delusion in the face of overwhelming evidence to the contrary—how very American. We want to believe that we should and we *will* come away the winner in the end. We will be one of the lucky ones.

Love to you,
Chris

January 27, 2023
New York, New York

MY FINGERS ARE CRAMPED AND sore, and my lower back needs stretching, the aftereffects of three hours spent stooped over, pulling English ivy out of the rocks and slopes of Central Park, just behind the statue of King Jagiello. I've been volunteering with the horticulture teams in Central Park for the last ten months or so, compensating for missing my garden, and I find I really enjoy engaging in mundane physical tasks that leave me with the satisfaction of visible accomplishment. In addition to its iconic buildings, meadows, and playing fields, the park comprises formal delineated gardens and "naturalized landscapes," the term of art for the product that Olmsted and Vaux deliberately sculpted to look primeval and eternal.

Our efforts today are directed at the Sisyphean task of removing invasive ivy. I grasp one tendril, pull, and get snagged on a mat of cross-woven vines that run in unexpected directions and grip the soil tenaciously. Each strand seems determined to run in multiple maddening diversions; at some point, I realize that the best approach is to combine pulling and cutting, snipping the strongest vines at key points, limiting the mass that can be extracted at any one time.

I'm thinking of the lives contained in the landscapes you experienced over the last week, the empty cliff dwellings below Thunder Mountain that seemed an abandoned Eden, the scent of avarice, lost hope, and defeat that imbued the abandoned mining town of Jerome,

Arizona. Those places still bear witness to human habitation, frailty, hope, and loss.

Central Park has existed as an artificial Eden for Manhattan for over 160 years—before then, it was not one iconic space but a patchwork of farms, reservoirs, forts, sheep pastures, and settlements, home to over one thousand people. The decision that was made in 1858 to uproot the few for the benefit of the many was perhaps emblematic of that peculiar American insistence on bending nature to its collective imagination, as well as disenfranchising those who have the least power to complain about it. Its past as a place where, for millennia, humans hunted, grazed their sheep, gathered pokeweed to extract ink from its berries, built homes, churches, taverns, and forts, all that has been deliberately and systematically erased. In their place, there is this harmonious elision of soft hills and valleys, spaces to dream, run, hit a ball, walk a dog, admire a vista, snap an iconic selfie, sit by a waterfall, observe the owls and hawks and ducks and sparrows, smile at the audacity of squirrels emboldened by generations of cohabitation with humans. It's a place where anyone can visit and exist on their own terms, for free, but where nobody has the right to stay and shape its contours to conform to their imagination.

The ivy represents the conceit of earlier generations of landscapers bent on recreating the grand European parks that inspired this one before anyone understood the long-term consequences of introducing species not native to a particular environment. Ivy is insidiously lovely, softening hardscapes and offering a green carpet in shaded corners where the winter ground might otherwise be brown and barren. But it is a brute that chokes out other species, splits rocks, and digs its tendrils into tree trunks. It spreads across the ground and climbs the oaks and hawthorns, a rooted, implacable constrictor bent on depriving the native species of access to sunlight and nutrients.

So, we are set to correct past errors and restore or create a new vision of the wholly artificial natural landscape based on the prevailing understanding of species cohabitation and preference for native flora. But oh boy, the ivy is tenacious. I have been watching the Netflix series *The Borgias* and indulged my imagination by endowing the ivy with the intelligence of that serpentine, shadowy, rapacious family. Jeremy Irons perfectly cast as the drawling, lazy-eyed, self-indulgent but shrewd Rodrigo Borgia, Pope Alexander VI (referred to as Sextus lest we miss the double entendre.)

It's quite a stretch to endow the plant with sentience, but uprooting it still seems a good metaphor for the messy and laborious work of facing the consequences of well-meaning decisions and for the futility of retracing life choices—hoping to pinpoint the moment when you made the fateful error and took the path that led you far from security, hope, fulfillment, and peace. There is no single vine that can be stripped, followed to its source, and named as the root of the error; it's all a matted tangle. The best we can hope for is to engage in our remediation with patient pruning and systematic effort, not shying away from the painful, stubborn knots, renewed with the clearer picture our efforts reveal.

These thoughts are close to the surface of my mind these days as I commemorate what would have been my son's twenty-fifth birthday by celebrating the exceptional soul he was while mourning the man I will never see. My conceit as a mother is to be tempted to believe that, at some level, I had control and simply failed to recognize the moment where I could have intervened, changed his perception, challenged his determination to end his life, and given him a reason to live. It's illusory, of course. Did I plant the ivy when I moved to Greece? When I raised my sons there? When I didn't insist on his moving to the States? When I took that last, fateful trip in October 2020?

And what would be lost if I were able to turn the clock back and live my life differently from one crucial point? I remember his first steps, his first words, milestones that had passed with his brother in expectant satisfaction. All kids walk and talk and ride bicycles, learn how to read and spell and recite the multiplication tables—with Greg, these steps were momentous and celebrated because their achievement was not a given. And my life has been far richer for the lessons of things hard-won, for the appreciation of small steps, for the savoring of minor victories.

As we turned in our tools, stretched our aching backs, and brushed off our knees, I looked back on the statue of Jagiello, King of Poland, Grand Duke of Lithuania, victor of the Battle of Grunwald in 1410, where he defeated the Teutonic aggressors. He holds two crossed swords in defiant celebration. The statue, a replica of one that stood in Warsaw, was part of the Polish exhibition of the 1939 World's Fair in Flushing Meadows. Jagiello was stranded in New York by the outbreak of WWII, and the original statue that he was modeled on was melted for munitions. New York Mayor Fiorello LaGuardia lobbied to keep the statue, apparently out of sympathy for the plight of Poland, and contributed a sum equivalent to its cost to the Polish war effort against the Nazis. What began as a symbol of national pride at an event designed to showcase all the peoples of the world became, once again, the embodiment of a nation's struggle for existence. I have admired him from the path that he guards, even as I have smirked a bit at the grandiose and musty pretense of bellicose equestrian statues in general. For much of the year, he is not visible from this vantage point, embraced in the dense foliage of the other seasons. Now, in the stark winter landscape, his back seems forlorn and heroic, besieged and determined. I muse at how many passersby will wonder how he came to be there, overlooking Turtle Pond below Belvedere Castle, one of the park's permanent mute residents. I wonder how many others ponder the palimpsest that is Central Park.

Weary but peaceful,

J

January 31, 2023
Breckenridge, Colorado

Y OUR IVY IS A TOUGH and intractable adversary and a metaphor for the tangles we make of our lives. I love how it wants to take over, to go where it should not go, but may also consent (for a while) to being trimmed and presentable. Alas, I fear I may have more than a little of an inclination to follow those creeping roots and vines, at times, asking why not? And, what if?

Today, at 6.30 a.m., I took a journey to the strange garden I must go to every two months. It lives inside the MRI machine at the university hospital in Denver.

After my brain surgery last April, I have undergone imaging every two months. Even with a hefty dose of Valium, I initially became extremely claustrophobic. Sheer terror overtook me each time I had to be rolled, flat on my back, head immobilized in a mask, into the narrow confines of the machine.

It was during my second session that I entered the garden.

In times of depression or great fear, a black jaguar has come beside me—emerging from my unconscious? The spirit world? —often joined by a large and rather sly looking snake. And now, eyes screwed tightly closed inside the MRI machine, I perceived the presence of these two animals. I lay rigid as if in a sarcophagus, as my ears split by the *bang bang bang* inside the metal tube. But then, my breathing relaxed slightly, my mind opened, and I followed the velvety shadow of Jaguar, the muscular undulations of Serpent to a place that was deeply green and lush, with all manner of plants: pungent and satiny, green and tall, turgid, extravagantly decorated with thorns and flowers. At the center of this place was a black, night-dark pond.

Here, the bellow of magnificent bullfrogs created the earsplitting sound, and the screeching that filled my head was made by fantastical herons, strange night birds, and the clattering wings of huge translucent dragonflies. I was no longer afraid; I was . . . curious. Hummingbird joined me, expanding in size and brilliance, urging me to awaken to life's sweetness even at this dire moment; Eagle soared above, drawing me up to fly wing-to-wing with the great spirit. *Yes*, I said. I can do this. I was no longer confined in a metal coffin, I moved freely through a loud and raucous nightscape full of color and texture and living energy.

Then, later in the morning, my oncologist, Dr. Ney, met with me and informed me that my results looked good. "Today, we celebrate," he encouraged me, smiling warmly. "Then, go out and keep doing what is important to you."

At home in Breckenridge, now, I tend to the plants that exist in this dimension, plants that are under my care. There are the geraniums that my aunt, living at a lower elevation, was going to discard at "the end of the season" one summer. This seemed so cruel! So, I adopted them. I love the earthy scent of their sensitive, fuzzy leaves, the way their pink and red flowers lean toward the sunny window. But they can only live inside—even in summer, it is too cold for them on the deck, in the shade, here at nearly ten thousand feet elevation. And when the sun does come out, its rays are so intense that the heat instantly dehydrates and flattens the poor leaves and blossoms.

Also living a carefully-tended indoor life is the poinsettia, given to me by my beloved Alan at Christmas the year I moved from Florida to Colorado. I could not bear to throw it out, and so the once-delicate poinsettia has grown from a holiday flower to a sturdy bush, with several trunks wrapped in silvery bark. Still, not nearly sturdy enough to spend time outside.

Finally, I anxiously care for my last Florida orchid. Every year in spring, it sends out a long stem that blooms with purple flowers. I do not know if this flowering is a final, desperate attempt at survival, or a sign that the orchid has happily settled into its strange mountain life by the window.

I love these plants and feel tremendously responsible for them—and fearful. I identify with them. Am I like these plants? Not meant to be living at 9,600 feet elevation and eight months of snow? How will they survive? How will I?

Today, my latest MRI came back with good results—all is normal. I consider the possibility that I should stop worrying about these plants, stop mourning the fact that life has changed (for them, for me) and that this change is not a sign of failure on my part. It is the nature of all things.

Instead, maybe I should care for them the best I can. But also acquire a plant or two that is tough, rambunctious and able to flourish under hard conditions. Maybe this future plant, like me, should embrace the good and the bad of living in such a climate, maybe I should stop feeling guilty about all the plants that I cared for at some other point in my life but which I cannot maintain in the Rocky Mountains. I could recognize that things have changed, but that I still survive.

And regarding this future plant, I am thinking that something thick-skinned and tough, spikey and a little dangerous might be just the thing.

Love,
Chris

February 8, 2023
New York, New York

YOU HAVE CONJURED A SELF-PROTECTIVE cocoon wrapped in semitropical color, clamor, and boisterous fecundity that embraced you through the bimonthly ordeal of the MRI. I cannot imagine the stress of having to submit to the machine's forbidding embrace, knowing that you must be still and stoic so that it can deliver your sentence—either a blessed but temporary reprieve or something too awful to envision. It seems crueler than necessary that the quality of your next two months of life is discerned by this cold, emotionless seer—a technological Pythia, impersonal and devoid of humanity. But you counter it with willful, conscious life. I imagine the machine, warmed by the tendrils of your conjured plants, the scampering of creatures and the echoes of their songs. And I love the idea of a thick-skinned, spiky, tough survivor as a new member of your plant tribe.

Our Wellesley classmate Lucy, my steady weekend walking partner, has long been urging me to choose one tree in the park as my avatar. After rejecting a number of London plane trees, majestic but indifferent, I have chosen the dawn redwood. There are three of them planted in Strawberry Fields, the section of Central Park adjacent to the west side 72nd Street entrance, across the avenue from the spot outside the Dakota where John Lennon was gunned down by the deranged fan back in 1981. (I remember exactly where I was—on the quad at Wellesley, after dinner, outside Pomeroy—when the news came that he'd been shot.) These days, I'm more likely to grimace at yet another earnest rendition of "Imagine" near the mosaic on the park sidewalk. But the story of the improbable resurrection of this nearly extinct species so captured my imagination that I had to find the tree, even if it meant braving the Sunday TikTok crowd.

I found myself standing at the base of a scraggly-looking trunk, and my irritation at the crowds dissipated. This species (scientific name *Metasequoia glyptostroboides*) is a weird conifer, a fast-growing deciduous tree native to China. It is ancient—it's present in the fossil record for the late Cretaceous period. In fact, it was identified as a fossil and assumed to be extinct in 1939; only two years later, a specimen was found growing in Hubei province, but as it was winter, no specimens were collected. (It is seriously sad looking in winter, devoid of needles—you could be excused for thinking it was dead.)

As the Second World War raged, teams of botanists, in defiance of or possibly indifferent to the chaos and uncertainty that permeated so much of life on the planet, kept sharing discoveries. They would have had to send letters, actual, physical, fragile letters—the fact that postal systems continued to function is an amazement in and of itself. At any rate, by 1948, *Metasequoia* was identified, recognized as having defied the war and the historical record and being, in fact, rare but very much alive. That same year, the Chinese botanists who had stayed in touch with their colleagues around the world, despite ideological divisions and political suspicions, collaborated with Harvard's Arnold Arboretum to collect and propagate seeds. The *Metasequoia*, this botanical coelacanth, was shared with a wider world. As it turns out, it's a very adaptable tree, happy when propagated in a variety of environments, including Central Park. This one, this scraggly, unprepossessing, weird misfit conifer, finally speaks to me for its improbable and enormously hopeful tale of survival. It tells me that people pay attention, they wonder, and they collaborate for the sheer beauty of things. Nobody patented it, bargained, or wheedled to obtain seeds—they simply shared the delight of discovery and the singular gift of watching a botanical dinosaur flourish. It tells me to look closely, to keep alive to a sense of wonder, to be slow to judge, and to be attuned to the stories things have to tell.

Here's to wonder,
J

February 19, 2023
Breckenridge, Colorado

D O I LOVE YOUR REFERENCES to Ancient Greek history and mythology so much because they have the effect of transforming my experience into something grand, worthy of consideration by the Oracle at Delphi? You allow me to imagine the possibility that even in these terror-filled moments in the basement of a medical facility before dawn, I am more than just a random collection of cells. I am more than "last name, date of birth, and insurance card," with an arm to be jabbed and an IV inserted to dye cells for contrast.

Instead, you lead me with a myth-enhanced torch out of this dark hole until I envision myself standing before the vast sweep of the ocean. Where my one story is a small but important flash of light and color in the tumble of waves that make up human history. There is Dread, and there may be Pronouncements of Doom, but they are announced with capital letters, and the experiences are those of someone who, even if briefly, sparkled. "Even if briefly" was important and mattered. Thank you.

Imagine. You scoff, I think, at how Lennon has been turned into a kind of TikTok prop. But that ridiculous commercialism doesn't take away from the meaning offered in his song. Consider how your ability to *imagine* has made me feel heroic rather than pathetic and insignificant as I face this terrible illness; consider how you have just *imagined* yourself into a whole new future with your job at the Central

Park Conservancy! Congratulations!

Your new job made me reflect upon my own career. Over thirty years, I imagined myself into a New York City businesswoman. I became a publisher in the field of commercial photography with expertise, leadership skills, an accumulation of important contacts in a bulging Rolodex, and the ability to get things done my way and to make a lot of money. I was proud of this successful career in New York and that I was able, eventually, to segue my skills into work as a consultant based remotely, first from the Adirondacks and then from South Florida.

But then, the housing crash that began in 2008, followed by divorce from my second husband, the implosion of my sales career, and the unexpected death of my father, landed me solidly in a state of financial and existential crisis. In a dramatic move that was perhaps cliché, *or just maybe* a great leap of the imagination, my next career shift was to become—at fifty-one-years old—a yoga instructor.

A chance weekend at Kripalu yoga center in the Berkshires introduced me to the possibility of being patient and forgiving at a moment in my life when I blamed myself ferociously for all my failures. Practicing yoga refocused my attention on a connection to nature, which I had neglected in my urban-centric business career. I resisted and then flourished in the unexpected intimacy of our training. Our class included around eight regulars and culminated with a trip to Peru in the Spring of 2012. The other students were younger, fitter, with more years of yoga training. We became friends, and the openness and acceptance of our small group persuaded me to let go of trying to live up to some harsh, imagined set of expectations.

Teaching yoga opened the door to an unexpected experience of grace. I had moved into a small one-bedroom apartment in Florida with my dog Luke and eliminated most expenses, but I had also gone through all of my savings and into debt. I had to make at least some money, and so I persisted day after day in trying to find a teaching position. But who would want a fifty-two-year-old yoga teacher?

A quiet lakeside community called Riverwalk hired me to teach "gentle yoga" for seniors three evenings a week. I don't quite understand this, but somehow, I was a natural. I put together playlists and sequences designed for older people or those with injuries. The Tuesday evening candlelight yoga class became a community favorite. I began to imagine that I could do this and came to love the regular students who attended my class and who inspired me to experiment with hands-on Reiki and guided meditations. Some students hired me for individual Reiki sessions, and I became a believer in the healing power of a caring touch. In time, I gratefully acknowledged that helping students in my classes to feel better, to move more easily, and to get a better night's sleep turned out to be the healing *I* needed.

In 2014, I reconnected with Alan, the person with whom I had competed, flirted, and nightly tied up our family's phone lines in ninth grade. How different and how much the same things were forty years later! I moved to Colorado, and I guess insecurity in this new relationship (with a *doctor*, a smart, important professional) led me to slip back into gunning for a job with an office and a respectable paycheck once again. For a while, I was development director at our local health clinic. However, I also began to write for the paper, and I did teach yoga for a while, although gentle yoga was never an easy sell in aggressive, sporty Breckenridge.

Just before my diagnosis last March, I had begun teaching again, this time leading a fall and then spring class of seniors in a workshop called "Writing the Stories of Your Life," with the tagline: "Your Story Is Important." I felt as if, once again, I had found a kind of calling through assisting others, particularly older people (now our age). As with my yoga classes, the students in these small groups generated a sense of sharing and intimacy. I felt blessed that I was able to imagine myself into this new role of offering a space in which individuals felt safe, inspired, and brave enough to "lead with their hearts."

Imagine. As a collective, we humans have not done a good job at imagining a more loving, more life-generating world. But it doesn't mean that we can't, right? As you say, sometimes "people pay attention, they wonder, and they collaborate for the sheer beauty of things." Imagine that.

May your new position at the Central Park Conservancy provide sacred space at this moment in your life for your own particular gifts to flourish. May you feel that what you have to offer is valued and appreciated. I for one value deeply your story of a very old pine tree and all the imaginings and the friendship that come with it.

Love and congratulations!
Chris

February 21, 2023
New York, New York

THIS PAST WEEK, I HAVE felt open to possibility.
A lot of this, as you can imagine, is colored by the rose-tinted elation of having gotten the Central Park Conservancy job. My old colleague at the Mediterranean Garden Society had emailed me on Monday to let me know that the recruiter had reached out to her for a reference and that she'd been effusive in response, which was nice to know, but I was still on tenterhooks. Then, Tuesday evening, my phone rang, and I saw the recruiter's name. A call is a good sign, as it's much easier to convey regrets via email, so I think I was smiling when I answered the phone. Excitement, relief and just joy—it felt as though the dislocation of the past few months, the ego blow of "failing" at my first foray back into the working world back in September, had resolved itself in my finding the thing I was meant to do.

The very next day, I went to an enrichment session for Park volunteers that I had signed up for a couple of weeks ago, and was met by the woman who had welcomed me as a volunteer last spring when I had turned to the park as not only my walking haven but also my garden. She had lived in Mykonos for many years, and we enjoy speaking Greek together. She was also my champion for this job, and is very likely the reason my weird résumé got pulled out of the virtual pile. Before the meeting, she quickly introduced me to her team, and I felt welcomed as a new colleague. The presentation on the history of the park resonated all the more, now that I would be in a position to share aspects of this with the general public.

The week continued with unexpected but welcome connections. I met a former colleague from my law firm days, a woman I hadn't seen for thirty years, for coffee. She had found me on LinkedIn, and we spent nearly three hours catching up. Our lives have taken very different trajectories, but there are some universalities of experience as women raising children and making choices, and we shared memories of the women partners at Rogers & Wells whose lives and choices had influenced our own.

That night, I went to hear Emmanuel Ax perform a Mozart piano concerto with the Orchestra of Saint Luke's. I happen to like this orchestra and I thought that I might not have many more chances to see Emmanuel Ax, so on a whim I booked a single ticket, treated myself to a glass of champagne, and made my way to my seat. I was up in the dress circle, one tier shy of the nosebleed seats, but in Carnegie Hall, that doesn't matter; the acoustics are amazing, and the whole stage is visible. There was one man in the aisle seat who stood to let me pass, and we made the usual polite noises.

I snuck a quick look at him, registering that he was about our age, looked neat and presentable but sort of dressed for a hike (more REI than Brooks Brothers, if you catch my drift), and that he had a white cane neatly folded in his lap. As the musicians settled themselves on stage, tuning, he rose slightly to take a picture. I remarked, "It's always beautiful, isn't it?"—really just to be polite, and to break the slightly awkward silence of two single people who are the only ones in the row and happen to be seated next to each other.

"It's my first time here—I live in Idaho." This began one of those memorable, heartfelt, fleeting exchanges that happen in travel, when you share surprisingly intimate things with a stranger precisely because you're not going to see them again, ever. His daughter lives in New York, and he and his wife have begun to visit multiple times per year, partly to see their child, but also because his wife is undergoing cancer treatment at Sloan Kettering. I can only wonder, and fear for her, how aggressive or unusual her cancer must be for her to endure the travel from Idaho to New York every two months—they have to drive to Jackson, Wyoming, then catch one flight to an interim hub, then another to New York. He hints at a full and interesting life—they've lived in Philadelphia, Washington, DC, and London at some point.

His vision is impaired, the result of a catastrophic stroke over fifteen years ago, which in turn was the freak result of an aneurysm that burst after a persistent coughing fit. He says this without self-pity, almost clinically, still marveling at the fact that something as simple as a cough could have triggered a cascade of events that caused him to have to relearn how to speak, see, walk. I tell him a little about my life as a native-born New Yorker who has returned for the third time, like a small planet with an erratic, slow orbit. I tell him, in a short, deliberately epigrammatic sentence, devoid (I hope) of drama or self-pity, that I came to New York this time to be with my surviving son after his brother's death by suicide.

Each of us, I believe, contemplated the other with genuine compassion for the seemingly random cosmic asteroids that had crashed into our lives, hurling our tidy little planets into spirals of grief, loss, bewildered pain, and incoherence. And we shared the hope of resilience, the realization that we were limping forward, finding our way, grateful for the touchstones we could grasp to hold steady.

It made me think of your healing journey with yoga and Reiki, and the immeasurable power of touch, whether it is physical or through compassionate attention. Touch, however rendered, is powerful enough to warrant reverence, I think.

We bonded over our appreciation of Central Park, a refuge into somewhere open, personal and vast, liberating in the anonymity it affords and comforting in the sense of fellowship it can also engender. I told him about my new job; he offered congratulations. We smiled at each other and exclaimed after Ax's encore, a piece of limpid, languid, slightly melancholy beauty. At the close of the concert, we shook hands, introduced ourselves by our first names, then separated, our evening made warmer by the momentary connection. I wish him well.

On Friday, I joined my weekly volunteer session, raking and gathering leaves in the Sheep Meadow with a group that was, coincidentally, only women. The weather was almost balmy—we worked in shirtsleeves, basking in the warmth of the winter sun. We are not friends, but we recognize one another from previous sessions, and share smiles and snippets of conversation. A lovely comradery develops when it's only women, most of us past fifty, some past seventy, as we hold bags open for each other, rake the spot where someone else's leaves have escaped in a swirl of wind, help drag the huge canvas-like bags over to the spot where the guy with the truck will pick them up, dump them, and return them to be refilled. I've observed that tourists are more likely to engage when they see women working, to ask questions, to praise our efforts; there were moments when I felt like part of the park experience, as though we were actors providing ambience. The previous week had been bitterly cold, and my team had been mostly men, the activity (shoveling compost) more muscular. The few visitors had hurried by, bent and muffled; nobody stopped to admire our diligence in turning an intimidating mound into a neatly spread blanket of nourishment for a stately old tree. I wonder how it will be when I am the uniformed park representative, how that will invite or discourage visitors to ask questions or directions. I'm excited to find out.

Carnegie Hall was followed by an outing on Saturday to a distinctly different performance in a Brooklyn distillery-cum-biker-bar with a guy I met through a matchmaking service and whom I've gone out with a couple of times. He had invited me to "Beethoven, Bach, Bops and Booze with Empire Wild and Orpheus." It was as random and interesting as it sounds, especially after I sampled their signature product, a sort of apple-based grappa of Slavic origins called *jablonka*. The "bops" portion turned out to include Celtic-sounding fiddle tunes, which recalled my experience with Greg in a pub in Kilkenny nearly four years ago, which made me wistful. It turns out I hadn't discussed Greg with him, which made our exit somewhat awkward. It's hard to smile and exchange polite inanities as you get into an Uber after you've just told someone that the basic reason you're in New York is that your son died by suicide. His reaction, to his credit, was kind and very empathetic.

And finally, as if my hyper-social week wasn't enough, I was invited to a small Super Bowl party at a family friend's apartment close by. I hadn't thought about the Super Bowl, or about professional football, since the last time I lived in New York. I found myself rooting for the Eagles (I liked their helmets) and enjoying the weirdly quintessential American feeling of the anthems, the fireworks, the ads, the halftime show, and yes, even the football.

I mix metaphors when I try to see myself in my journey between before and after. I sometimes feel more like an orbiting object, whose unpredictable trajectory enables both chance encounters and dizzying dislocation, and sometimes more as a living organism seeking its soil. I spent many years tenaciously forming roots in the arid, alkaline, austerely harsh soil of my adopted land, finding beauty in the particular pungency of endurance. I identified with the salvias, their beautiful variations of flowers complemented by their tough, furry, resilient foliage. Then, my roots were torn raw from that place, wary of trusting a new placement. I am tentatively, literally, returning to my roots, to my native soil.

Can we be both? Ethereal, heaven-bound, and rooted, grounded in place and heart? I think so. Your native garden, in many ways, seems to be the semitropical lushness of Florida, where plants and beasts flourish in color, noise, heat, and richness, the possibilities of reinvention. Colorado can seem harsh, yet you've found ways to protect the fragile non-natives, embrace the tough things that flourish there, and celebrate the small, resilient, miraculous flowers. May it embrace you as one of its own, daunted but strong despite the challenges, alive to the wonder as well as the beauty.

Today, as I walked in the park, the witch hazel on Cedar Hill was in bloom. It is said to be the harbinger of spring, and its spiky, butter-yellow flowers seem too fragile for this February weather. But it's a tough, useful, multi-talented shrub with powerful anti-inflammatory and antiviral properties. We always had a bottle of witch hazel extract in our medicine cabinet when I was growing up, and I loved its weird, distinct scent. Maybe this will be my new plant persona, a complement to my ancient tree—hopeful, brave, useful and a little bit weird.

Thanks for being a friend who's not afraid of my weirdness,
Love,
J

February 22, 2023
Saint John, USVI

Y OUR DESCRIPTION OF YOUR ENCOUNTER with the man at the
concert spoke so eloquently of human suffering, dignity and
courage. You were like two travelers walking together for this brief
moment, sharing kindness and encouragement. And isn't that one
of the most valuable gifts we can offer each other in this life?

Above all I felt a sense of joy in your bubbly flow of episodes:
receiving "the call" and getting the job, connecting with old friends,
the poignant encounter at the concert, bagging leaves at the park,
an all-American Super Bowl party. And so, my mind went to writing
something that also connected a number of short scenes or vignettes,
as you will see.

I got a little teary at your question, "Can we be both? Ethereal,
heaven-bound, and rooted, grounded in place and heart?" So often,
I am torn between these two seemingly opposite poles, not knowing
what the answer is. But you made me laugh with that final characterization of yourself as "hopeful, brave, useful, and a little bit weird." I
love every one of these traits in you!

I write now toward the end of a magical trip to Saint John, where
we joined Alan's mother, his sisters, and their spouses for a celebration of his mom's ninetieth birthday. We gathered in Saint Thomas,
in the Virgin Islands, wrangling suitcases at the airport and track-
ing down our rental cars, then boarding the car ferry to Saint John.

Alan's mother, Elinor, had announced to us last July that she wanted to spend her birthday somewhere warm where she could snorkel.

Alan's family on holiday, it soon became clear to me, could be characterized as a collection of generals, each with a very specific battle plan for how to enjoy a tropical vacation. Perhaps I was pursuing my own strategy. By testing positive for COVID on the third day of vacation, I avoided altogether the ensuing family skirmishes over beach selections and restaurant choices, spending most of my time on the outdoor terrace of our large Airbnb on Cruz Bay, observing life around me or slipping into the ocean for a swim.

Temperatures ranged in the low eighties; a constant, gentle breeze rustled through the leaves of the seagrape, and—as the two cars carrying Alan's boisterous family pulled out of the driveway for the day—the rhythmic tossing of the waves on the beach below our terrace lulled me into a near trancelike state of wonder. That I am still here among the living, that I was able to experience this family gathering in this beautiful place was a miracle to me. I offer a collage of impressions.

Observations from an Island Terrace

We arrive at a house by the sea with an island terrace where a brief downpour falls across the sun-shot water, the waves rippling beneath the rain like a cloth woven of silver threads ready to part and reveal the answer to a mystery. I've lived these sixty-one years greedily wanting to fit so many lives into one, and still, it doesn't feel like enough.

The peacock proceeds with measured step around the outer edge of the stone wall surrounding the terrace. He examines the seagrape berries, plucks one, then marches along the shoreline, trailing his royal train of feathers while long toes grip the large beach rocks and hunks of coral. Up the small path he climbs and arrives on the terrace. He angles his tufted head and eyes with interest the cracker and cheese in my hand. Then, his foot snaps up to give his chin a nonchalant scratch.

I might challenge you, tiny green lizard with the yellow stripe, watching me from the wall on which we both are perched. I might dispute the assertion in your appraising stare, should you voice your thoughts (which you seem quite capable of doing). Your dark bulging eyes announce, *Don't underestimate me! I wasn't born yesterday, you know!* Is that so, small lizard not even two inches long?

As a group, we humans have planned and debated over this trip for months. Which tropical location would have the best beaches, snorkeling, restaurants? But now, having examined the property and its features, selected rooms, and unpacked suitcases, we struggle to actually be here. Can we let go of the habit of talking and asserting ourselves or of shifting all our attention to our cell phones, tablets, laptop computers? Can we arrive fully in this place?

What? What was that? A large bottle-green hummingbird darts so fast through the air that—though he is nowhere near me—I duck. Sitting up again, I peer into the foliage from which he emerged; now, sipping nectar from the delicate sprays of flowers is a bananaquit, a cheery chuckling warbler, yellow as a banana with a curved beak like a handy straw.

The clank of the bell around her neck is muffled beneath the goat's distressed bleating. Is she lost? I worry. But in this small neighborhood with its rutted, slow-driving side roads and overgrown pink bougainvillea, could she really be lost? She cries out again, and from a grassy hillside farther down the beach from our house comes the answering baaaas and bleats. She springs across the stones to join a motley herd of goats of all sizes. Later, they return as one jumbled, bell-clanging group trotting in front of the terrace, sampling the seagrape berries. Happy, I think, to be together. No goat wants to be left behind.

Watch out for the chickens! Brown, white, black-speckled, and from tiny to medium to large in size. They dash between bushes, across the road, in front of cars, each somehow managing not to trip over the chicks darting to and fro between their scaly feet. Into the fray sprints a rooster or two. The cocks have been up since 3:24 a.m., shouting at each other. Which I know because I sleep with the bedroom window open.

Just above the horizon line of the ocean, the pelican sails in front of the house, back and forth, all day long. Wings held out at his sides, his body rigid as a spear tip. Then, an arrow-like plunge into the water for prey. Returning to the surface, he is all loose and flapping and shaking his fish-filled crop. Pleased with himself, he waggles his tail feathers.

We are not good at being still or unoccupied, at observing and permitting the world to move on its axis without trying to intervene or to seek other distractions. Will we pay enough attention to the rustling of birds and lizards in the green leaves, the smell of sea and the taste of salt on our skin and the peace of white puffy clouds in an azure sky so that these things become a part of us, memories embedded in who we are?

How does the hermit crab know that I have stepped onto the terrace? My arrival prompts him to pause. How does he know that if he creeps diagonally across the tiles and toward the outside wall, he will reach an opening meant to drain rainwater? When he approaches this tiny semicircle, much smaller than combined crab and shell, how is it that the hermit crab believes he can escape through this drain hole? After several moments of stillness, all his many legs retract, and his spiral shell slowly lowers. With a slight tipping forward, the crab enters the hole and disappears. I run to examine the opposite side of the wall, where the drainpipe exits. The hole is just too small—surely, he is stuck now. But moments later, a collection of legs emerges and—pop!—he drops to the ground on the other side and scuttles off into the thick leaves and stems of the seagrapes.

Sending you warm breezes and whispers of spring,
Chris

Spring

March 4, 2023
New York, New York

YOUR LETTER WAS A DELIGHT for the senses, a series of acutely executed miniatures that whimsically explore the inner lives of other creatures. I firmly believe that animals have emotional lives—that the goats bleat more contentedly when they are all together, that the clucks that accompany the chickens' scurrying are their equivalent of morning gossip, like mothers on the playground. The lovely conceit of being judged by the lizard or outsmarted by the spatial awareness of the hermit crab made me smile.

The happy, unexamined existence of the animals contrasted starkly with the humans, whose discomfort with the need to navigate unfamiliar physical closeness and balance their competing priorities seems to have led them to swerve away from moments of connection. Emotional interaction for people whose principal connection is blood rather than choice can be as chancy as a walk through a minefield, and I can understand the temptation, whether conscious or not, to stay on the edges and avoid the bold plunges that can lead to explosions.

But what a delight it is to have time to observe, to make your only task, for a few minutes, to pay attention, to embroider the observations with the colors of the sky, the seagrape leaves, the sparkle of rain on water, the contrast of sea and sunset. By naming the elements of the moment, you savor them, much as you note and name the flavors when you roll a mouthful of wine around before swallowing. Some moments are for gulping, but it's lovely to have ones that are sipped.

My first two weeks of work have been a wonderful adventure. The only universal characteristic of my new colleagues is their kindness—they all help without judgment, give advice on things I might encounter, and point out the stumbling points before I have a chance to stumble. Their profiles are wildly disparate—Bronx natives with ten or more years of experience working in the park; Gen Zers younger than my son, from Arkansas and Upstate New York, looking for literary inspiration or a break for their indie rock band; people my own age in a second or third career; and one colleague who is kind, far from sane, and an absolute delight.

The day can be very different depending on where I work, and I look forward to discerning the different energies emanating from the four locations. The Dana Center, in the far northeast corner of the park, is the newest, a product of the stewardship of the conservancy, which decided to replace a burned-out boathouse and build a place that would extend the sense of park as a sanctuary of community for New Yorkers. Before the conservancy assumed the operation of the park, very few visitors ventured further north than the reservoir, and the absence of appeal for tourists had enabled the city's tendency to devote fewer resources to local residents. It's quiet in the winter, but the visitors are mostly locals, and their delight in their park is palpable.

Designed in homage to Calvert Vaux's distinctive Victorian Gothic architecture, the Dana has a fairy-tale feel—a steeply-pitched slate roof, red and green gingerbread woodwork buttressing its portico. It's a nature center, where kids can fish in the Harlem Meer on spring and summer weekends and learn to identify the turtles, birds, fish, and frogs that abound. A little boy came in with his father on a blustery Sunday and asked for the leaflet that identifies the fish species in the Meer—five minutes later, he burst back in the door and announced, "I think I saw a *carp!*"

The other center where I've now worked is the Dairy, close to the zoo and the skating rink near the bustling south end of the park. The visitors are mostly tourists, happy to find a gift shop, asking directions to the nearest restroom and advice on must-see spots in the two hours they've allotted to the Central Park experience. But here, too, connections can be made—a favorite topic is Flaco, the renegade Eurasian eagle owl who escaped from the zoo after persons unknown cut open his enclosure, and who has defied expectations and captured imaginations as he reinvents himself as a genuine park resident. As you observed the birds and beasts great and small on Saint John, imbuing them with traits of curiosity, boldness, and purpose, so do we identify bravery and cunning in Flaco and take pride in his resourcefulness.

The work days, then, are full of fleeting connections that warm and please me; quieter, more reflective connections are made on my volunteer days. My current work schedule has left me available on the days when the volunteer opportunities are the more prosaic "maintenance" tasks, a nice way of saying that we pick up trash. This is less communal than the horticulture teams, as each of us slowly trolls a patch of ground, alert to the cigarette butts, torn-up lottery tickets, granola bar wrappings, beer bottles, and less savory droppings. At the picnic tables near the pinetum just below the reservoir at 86th Street, the detritus is largely benign; further north, up on the heights near 102nd Street, we have found discarded needles, broken bottles, and the occasional crack pipe.

I've learned to move slowly, combing the same small patch from different angles, suddenly spotting a bottle cap or paper bag scrap that was invisible from another perspective. It's oddly meditative, as it drives you to focus all your attention on the small patch in front of you—the satisfaction of spotting a hidden item is as genuine as it is absurd.

Solitary as this activity can be, there is a ray of connection in this exercise in the person of the ebullient Alabama transplant who is the second in command on garbage patrol. A cross between Johnny Appleseed and Mr. Rogers, he sprinkles every address with "yes, ma'am" or "yessir" naturally and unselfconsciously; it's absolutely endearing. He's also a keen observer with a poetic soul who savors the stories told by the trash. Five Marlboro butts, smoked down to the filter, next to one half-smoked Virginia Slims cigarette; she left abruptly, perhaps after a fight, and he stayed moodily smoking, replaying the conversation gone wrong in his mind. I found a rat skull, as startling and perfect as the antelope skulls in a painting by Georgia O'Keeffe—I offered it to the trash boss, who accepted it with delight. We've talked about the drama and poignancy that trash vignettes can contain and mused on the fact that most of what anthropologists know about the ordinary people who lived, flourished, and died over the eons is derived from sorting through the things they discarded.

That week was punctuated by a brief trip to DC, where I spent most of Monday and Tuesday with my sister, but I also saw two other women friends, Robin and Claudia, for dinner Monday night. I have known Claudia for over twenty years. She is a good friend and the vice president of the American College of Greece, where Greg was a philosophy student. She was instrumental in placing a bench in his memory at a campus spot he loved. I was shown the spot in 2021 by one of Greg's friends and classmates who, as a good Muslim, would pray five times a day; he had chosen the spot because it's at a high point and orienting himself toward Mecca was easier. Greg was an avowed atheist but a good friend and would keep him company. I met Robin through Claudia about eight years ago in Athens, when Robin's husband was working for the IMF and Greece was still on financial life support. I brought Robin into the orbit of the Mediterranean Garden Society, where she now serves on the board.

Since then, both Claudia and I have divorced, and Robin's husband faces the same bleak diagnosis as you, lagging about four months behind. He, too, spends his days living life to the fullest, traveling, playing tennis, and seems to accept that which he cannot change without too much existential worry.

I looked at us, considering how much each of us has been buffeted and how marvelous it is that we can still see each other and appreciate the women we are, even as the core is tested by heat, pain, loss, and fear. I read something the other day that seemed apt: "Remember that everyone you meet is afraid of something, loves something, and has lost something."

My train home was jogging along merrily when we came to a halt outside Trenton—the official announcement was that we would be stopped for at least an hour and a half, and updates would be given as available. There was a collective exhalation of irritation, and as we pulled partway into the station, allowing passengers to disembark, I thought of joining the majority who were busy organizing group Ubers into the city. Then I heard the conductor quietly explain to another passenger the reason for the delay—someone had ended their life on the tracks, jumping in front of the train that immediately preceded ours.

My first thought was a silent prayer for the family, for their last moments of careless wholeness, for the wave of shock, sorrow, grief, and pain that would slam into them from behind, hurling them into the sand and stones of the shallows, panicked and disoriented, struggling to right themselves and make sense of it all. From my current perspective, I now know that they will, to some extent, be okay. There will come a day when the raw grief is not the only sensation they can feel, where they can smile at a cheeky squirrel or small child and not feel a guilty sting for betraying their grief. There will come a day when they can give in to joy and wonder. But there will always be moments, like this one was for me, when the sensations and emotions rush back, when I was not curled to protect my heart, and the slam of the shock feels as fresh and as violating as it did the night Greg ended his life. I did not find out any details, respecting the person whose life had ended, but I sent another silent prayer that they might be at peace. I did, however, decide that dinner on the train could consist of a half-bottle of Cabernet and a bag of potato chips. I thought of pouring out a libation but decided it was overdramatic.

The next day, I once again found refuge working at the Belvedere Castle, chatting with colleagues, directing visitors, and watching the thuggish Canada geese drive the lovely northern shoveler ducks off Turtle Pond. The Wednesday crew included several colleagues I had not worked with before; this made me as nervous as the first day of school, but it was fine. On Friday, I worked again with my kookiest colleague, who decided that the squirrel who lives in the tree hollow in front of the conservancy kiosk in Columbus Circle speaks Italian and is named Benedetto. Some connections fray slowly, others rupture violently, but there are new connections, the soft tendrils that help heal the raw ends.

I hope spring in Saint John is kind to you,
Love,
J

March 13, 2023
Breckenridge, Colorado

R ooted, grounded in place and heart. I've been thinking about your words from a few letters back. Now, the descriptions you give of your first days working in Central Park evoke a wonderful feeling of being grounded, of finding peace and simple pleasures with your new colleagues in a place that is beautiful and packed with interesting history. It could be that after all the recent upheaval and stress in your life, the sense of peace you experience on the inside allows you to calm down enough to see things more clearly—and with greater pleasure—on the outside. It seems to me that you are feeling at home.

Home is a tricky concept, isn't it? What is *home*?

After a weekend in Moab, Utah, Alan and I drove along the Colorado River, heading back to Breckenridge. Our home. The towering red cliffs of this awesomely beautiful place looked down on us, but their spirits seemed preoccupied with deeper matters than one more car loaded down with mud-caked mountain bikes. I was drowsy and sore after riding, and my thoughts wound their way back to our correspondence and back to Scarsdale, the town where you and I grew up.

Me, an angry and resentful teen, feeling thwarted, patronized, and limited by my parents' views of the world. My mother, more and more provoked as I challenged her authority.

"As long as you live under *our* roof, you will do what we say!" she snapped at me during one of our battles. "Otherwise, you can pack your bags and leave!"

I shot back, "This is my home too!"

In a fury, she corrected me: this house was, in fact, my parents' home *first and foremost*, as it was my father who paid all the bills—not me.

I challenged her. "But how are you any different from me?" If it was not my house, it certainly wasn't hers either because it was Dad, not her, who worked and who paid for things!

My insolence earned me a slap across the face.

An insecurity wormed its way inside of me from that time forward. On some level, the places I had thought of as "home"—our house in Scarsdale, the country house in New Hampshire with the long front porch that faced the mountains—were not really mine, not "my home" in the way I had understood them to be. Mom and Dad could eject me from these places of comfort, safety, and family life without my agreement at any time.

Would my mother have really been fine with that? Kicking me out? It had never occurred to me before that I might not belong in this house, with this family—with Mom and Dad, my little sister and brother, the dog, and the cat. I took the threat at face value and was shaken that my parents could be willing, it seemed, to consider this possibility. My mother hardened in her resolve ("Shape up or ship out!"); my father reacted with anger and frustration at the disruption of the family by his eldest child.

Another kid my age might have reacted with a resentful "Harrumph!" Or met up with friends to rebelliously smoke some weed and commiserate about parents. That kid might then have simply forgotten about the whole thing. But not me. Slowly, I became unmoored. And with my storytelling mind, I began to create an idea of myself as having *no home.*

But that was okay, right? I wanted to see the world. Home, after all, represented all that was restrictive and the ever-present possibility of me doing something wrong. I took my first, very loosely "school supervised," overseas trip to Scotland and Greece at sixteen and confounded my parents by becoming engaged, briefly, to a Scottish bus driver. I spent a semester of college in France. Travel—sometimes very distant travel—became a part of my life.

For many years, my work necessitated living out of hotel rooms in Italy, Tokyo, Hong Kong, and Washington, DC. Sometimes I found long hotel stays a relief from the complicated notion of "home." For one thing, rooms in hotels were comfortable, often came with a great view when I traveled internationally, and were invariably bigger than my apartment in New York City. But more importantly, the temporary and anonymous nature of hotel living forestalled any uneasiness around possible rejection and loss.

Once, wondering if I could settle down in any of these places, I asked a friend of mine in Hong Kong, "Where is *home* for you?" Graham was an expat British photojournalist. He had a tiny, bare room of an apartment and spent much of his time away, traveling and shooting. He thought about it for a while and responded, "I'm home inside myself."

I wished I could feel that way.

In the forty years after leaving Scarsdale, I have lived and tried to create "home" in various apartments in New York City, a cabin in the Adirondacks, a house with a pool in Florida, and now in Breckenridge, Colorado. So often in the past, the places I thought I could embrace as home eventually stopped feeling that way. I'd end up seeing myself as an outsider, bored or alienated and uneasy. It's almost as if I'd insist on standing apart from others because to be cast out, rejected would be far worse.

So many decades after those childhood battles with my parents, why can't I experience, with confidence and certainty, the sense of really being home?

Alan and I lie in bed the next morning after our return from Utah. It's cold, and neither of us wants to get up or go out. But we need a few items from the store.

"I have to get a refill of those vaginal estrogen pills." I sigh. It's silly, but I feel slightly embarrassed when the young, male pharmacy tech hands me a prescription that makes it clear that *I*, an almost sixty-two-year-old woman and perhaps old enough to be his grandmother, am still *doing it*.

"We need more lube, too," Alan adds. He does not have the same inhibitions I do.

I groan. "Oh, great. Which one of us old folks is going up to the counter to purchase that stuff? Also, we need mustard."

"And soap."

This list is getting too long. I complain, "Why do we need *more soap*?"

"To wash all that mustard off of our bodies!" He rolls over and grabs me in bed.

"Whaaaaat?!" I squawk and can't help cracking up. I let him wrap his arms around me, this man I have known since we were both children, thirteen and fourteen years old. For a moment, I understand that this ridiculous conversation is a message from the universe: though it has taken me a very long time to get here, I am, in fact, home. (The mustard, by the way, is for sandwiches).

Not long before my mother passed away, I brought up with her the conversation we had had so many years earlier, in which she had threatened to kick me out of the house. She was pretty ill by then, and I hope I asked about this gently.

"Oh, that," she took a sip of her tea as we sat together at her kitchen table in Florida. And she thought for a moment. "You were such an easy kid when you were little, *Chrissy-winkle*. And so difficult as a teenager! I'm sure I was at my wits' end!" She tilted her head, which I chose to understand as a nod to regret at our struggles. Then she smiled and laid her hand on top of mine. "Of course, I didn't mean it."

Looking forward to yours,
Chris

March 21, 2023
New York, New York

Y OUR STRUGGLES TO FEEL AT home in various places were echoed in my life this past week. Is that by chance, I wonder, or are we connected by energy?

As I think I've told you, my trip to Greece last summer was unsatisfying and alienating. Athens in July is unnaturally quiet, as many residents seek respite from the relentless heat by escaping to the islands or the remote villages their grandparents came from. I was able to see a number of my friends, but everyone was on their way somewhere. I went to Tzia, an island very close to Athens, to attend a wedding and then to the island of Skyros; in both places, I felt off-kilter. Despite having an Athenian refuge in the home of my friend Valeria, where I slip into ease, as cozy as a hand in a glove, I left Greece feeling unsettled. I had lived in Greece for thirty years and spoke the language well enough to fool people on the phone into believing that I was Greek. (One look at my freckled Irish face in person belies that and led to some startled looks over the years.) How was it possible that I could feel like I didn't belong, like I'd put my shoes on the wrong feet?

This feeling of dislocation was compounded by my hasty six-day visit in November, when my psychological state was at a very low ebb in any case, and where half the time was spent winding up my duties as the general secretary of the Mediterranean Garden Society. The MGS was the only "expat" activity I had taken part in during my time in Greece; I had spent many happy days over the years working in the magical garden at Sparoza with Sally, an indomitable Anglo-Irish widow in her eighties whose upper-crust drawl and fantastical life made it feel like I was having tea with a character from a Kipling novel. My love for this garden and the people I had met there had led me to agree to this final three-year term on the board; during that period, my world had shattered and split into shards like a glass dropped on a stone floor, and I was ready to be done with it. I barely had the energy for a few stolen moments to see a very few people, including that sad hour-long lunch with my wasband.

All of this is to say that I fully understood your sense of despair at truly belonging somewhere. I'm trying to reinvent myself as a New Yorker on my third lifetime iteration of living in the same Manhattan neighborhood. It's certainly not the city's fault since New York, perhaps more than other cities, grants permission to anyone to identify themselves as a legitimate resident. I still have occasions when I feel a bit of a fraud despite the deep connections; happily, my new job has given me a much greater sense of legitimacy and purpose that is profoundly affirming.

But I had a recent experience that affirmed I did once belong in Athens. I woke up about ten days ago to a WhatsApp group chat from my "forum" friends in Athens, talking about getting together for dinner. This group is a loose coalition of seven women who met monthly to share just about everything about our lives for over fifteen years. We range in age from sixty-four to forty-five, so our life phases overlap but are not synchronized. We had stopped meeting regularly before I left Greece, but we would still get together a couple of times per year to catch up, share progress of kids and marriages and divorces, laugh, cry, and enjoy each other's company. I have particular friendships with several of the women, but all of them were there for me when I separated, and when Greg died.

After reading through the plans that had developed while I slept, I joined the chat—can I be included? Can you add me to part of the dinner via video call? It was enthusiastically arranged, and last Tuesday, I joined the dinner party by phone. For the next hour and a half, we laughed, shared gossip, told stories of what we'd all been up to, talked about how we felt to have aging spouses (or not), welcomed a first grandchild, and commiserated about kids still in early high school, adult children and family business succession troubles, sex lives and menopause. It was wonderful. I got off the phone as they all headed home past midnight, still warmed by the glow of the friendship, and mentally chastised myself for having doubted the enduring power of this friendship.

That same evening, I had been invited to the home of a Greek-American acquaintance to welcome a Greek actor whose TV series had been syndicated worldwide by Netflix, a first for Greece and, thus, a notable accomplishment. I had responded that I would come, but as the hour approached to dress, I was once again seized by self-doubt. I wouldn't know anyone there. I would dress wrong. I was only invited out of pity. It's okay; I can always leave early. Just put on contacts, mascara, and lipstick; it'll be fine. This is stupid; it's really cold out; I might not find a cab to come back.

And yes, I went. I knew plenty of people who were happy to see me. I had a wonderful time, and I made a mental note to remember this the next time I felt that an invitation was not really for me. I also realized, by seeing the way the Greeks far from home interacted with one another, that I had given up so much by moving to Greece just in terms of human connections with people who knew me from a hatchling. The Greeks in New York stay in touch, get together, and stay connected to who they were when they were kids through these friendships. I made very few "expat" friendships during my first twenty years in Greece, partly out of my determination not to be the foreign wife and partly out of my ex's determination to subsume me into his life, his friends, their wives, and all things Greek. Much of the appeal of the MGS was the weekly chance to garden in a beautiful space and then share "pudding" (Sally's very Victorian upper-crust term for sweets of any kind) with other ladies who had chosen Greece but remained very much American, English, or Australian.

So, on to death. I have gotten into the habit of signing up for or getting tickets for things as soon as they appeal to me even a little, on the theory that I should be open to new experiences, and if the day arrives, and I don't feel like going, there's little harm done. On that principle, I had gotten myself a ticket to the opening of an exhibit on, well, death, at the Rubin Museum, a smallish but still impressive space in Chelsea dedicated to understanding Buddhism and its crossover with Hinduism in the Nepal/Tibet/Bhutan area. As the day approached, I thought of including the guy I met through the matchmaking service, and he gamely agreed to make a Friday evening trek into Manhattan.

I got there almost an hour before he did and had the chance to see the exhibit and enjoy the space, which was very convivially arranged and felt more like a party than a museum. There were liberal pours of wine at the bar, a DJ spinning good music, and a table offering temporary tattoos. It felt like an almost festive, jolly way to approach death as a part of life, a stage rather than an end, which I gather is kind of the whole point of this religious approach.

I had had a full glass of rosé on a largely empty stomach and was feeling happily buzzed when I went over to the tattoo table. A businesslike man asked where I wanted it placed, and I chose the inside of my right forearm, just under the white ink tattoo I had gotten in 2017, after my separation, that reads "What's past is prologue." He slapped the sticker down, covered it with a wet paper towel, and enjoined me to make sure it was thoroughly wet and to hold it in place for at least thirty seconds. I happily complied, and, within a minute, peeled off the backing to reveal what the mystery message might be.

The tattoo read: "Death is not the end." Hardly surprising, given the theme of the exhibition. And yet it shot through me like a jolt of electricity. It felt intensely personal, mystically directed to me from Greg, even as the analytical part of my brain tried to persuade me that it was entirely predictable and unremarkable. I tried to steady my heart, to name and feel each of the emotions I was experiencing. Shock, love, fear, longing, and simple, profound sadness, missing him with an intensity that left me short of breath. Disoriented, I found a place to sit, and ended up chatting with a stranger before participating in a chant led by a saffron-robed lama Rinpoche. My date arrived, we went through the exhibition at some speed, then retreated to a nearby Italian restaurant. I didn't tell him what I had experienced with the tattoo, but we did talk a bit about loss—his sister had died of COVID in late 2020.

All of this got me thinking about the energy of connection and love, which tied into the discussions you and I have had about *mati*, the Greek (and Arabic, and Turkish, but never tell them it's all the same thing) conception of the evil eye, or bad energy that can have deleterious effects on one's health and well-being. It can be warded off by wearing a blue eye amulet or, in case it's been imposed, removed through the intercession of someone who can *xematiazei* or take away the bad energy through directed prayer. I have no idea why this should work, nor any understanding of the intersection of belief and the placebo effect, but I have seen it "work" under circumstances that left me little doubt of its effectiveness, so I am a cautious believer. And I wear two *mati* bracelets, although I do not spit and make the sign of the cross when giving a compliment; I guess this is a Western compromise.

And I will happily believe that the energy of love and the desire to protect and celebrate those I love has an invisible but potent force. Shortly after Greg's death, someone sent me a beautiful piece by the physicist Aaron Freeman called "Why You Want a Physicist to Speak at Your Funeral." Freeman explains that, according to the first law of thermodynamics: "No energy gets created in the universe, and none is destroyed . . . all [the] energy, every vibration, every BTU of heat, every wave of every particle that was [my] beloved child remains in this world."

His lovely, comforting words end with this thought: "According to the law of the conservation of energy, not a bit of you is gone; you're just less orderly."

I believe that, and also believe that some of that energy is infused with love.

Love,

J

April 1, 2023
Breckenridge, Colorado

L AST WEEK'S MRI, WITH ITS good results, sent me briefly soaring into clear blue skies of relief. I texted the news to friends and their happy replies flew back to me; I felt as if those messages might confirm for me, once and for all, that everything is really going to be all right. But shortly after I fell back to earth, crawling around in blind anger. I'll have to go through all of this terror again! In just two more months! Since last week, I've been trying to haul myself back up onto my feet. Just walk. Just put one foot in front of the other.

I spend much of my time in the small, comforting world of my relationship with Alan. He has taken on so much of the responsibility for dealing with doctors, the insurance company, the frustratingly endless calls when there is some scheduling issue. He takes the lead on all our joint financial responsibilities like taxes and shuttles me around from place to place. I am deeply grateful for his help . . . and, at times, deeply resentful for my loss of independence. I hate the scattered nature of my thinking these days, how hard it can be to pay attention, the way I miss things in emails and texts, and the slow speed with which I complete any task involving reading. Sometimes, I am, frankly, just a bitch to be around.

But above all, I am conscious every day of my deep pleasure in his company. I have been bored, restless, afraid, or disengaged in every one of my previous relationships. With Alan, it is so easy and natural to joke around; we love our walks as much as our time on the couch. We have gleefully revived our "Who is smarter?" competition, which began in ninth grade when, at Scarsdale High School, my IQ was determined to be one point higher than his. This rivalry currently expresses itself in trying to beat each other at the *New York Times* Spelling Bee each morning. At the end of the day, I look forward to the animal comfort of snuggling up in bed together. Sometimes, I reach out and slide my fingers between his. Or he turns toward me and lays his palm across my heart, a tenderness which sends me right to sleep.

The opposite pole of my daily existence is grappling, as best as I am able, with what it means to be aware that death may be very close by. How do I make peace with those I've experienced conflict with? With myself? Is it foolish, egotistical, to want to get one more book published, to leave something of who I am behind? I want a sense of completeness in my life—but is that possible? Necessary? What is on the other side?

And then there is this place in the middle, between the closeness of married life and the loneliness of trying to Solve the Questions of the Universe. Ordinary day-to-day life among the people we know. Oh, yeah—that. In the past weeks, I'd forgotten about that.

You reminded me about this part of life with your recent story of making the effort to join your women friends in Greece, via Zoom, even as a little satellite in far-off Manhattan. I have had to think about your surprisingly satisfying experience at the cocktail party with other Greek friends and acquaintances, despite your initial reluctance.

We received tickets to a fundraising event on Saturday, and neighbors had invited us to dinner on Sunday. But did I really want to be out among people? In a big group, people might all feel sorry for me, uncomfortable, or have forgotten about me completely. And what if

I just got overwhelmed? In a neighbor's home, would Alan and I feel like we are under the microscope?

What a pleasure it turned out to be, to arrive as a guest to an event that—once upon a time when I was development director at the local health clinic—I used to be in charge of! Now, Alan and I hung out with the crowd of tipsy "old locals": retired doctors, nurses, and ski instructors, former clinic staff who these days work part-time or volunteer, and a number of people who seemed to know me as the local Summit County author. How nice! In just a few years, we've all grown weatherworn here in the mountains and old enough for the younger crowd to take over. Rushing around importantly, the next generation gave orders and made sure we old folks didn't pinch any free drinks and that we moved from the bar to our seats in the dining area in a timely manner for the fundraising event. Later, when the band started up, I kicked off my high heels, and Alan and I forgot about being old and joined the dance party.

On Sunday, we had dinner in the neighborhood with a couple and their two teenage sons. Both the kids have helped us, over the years, with pet-sitting, plant watering, log stacking, and other chores. I feel a sense of possessiveness toward them—*my* neighborhood boys. We have had the pleasure of watching them grow up, the surprise at seeing the eldest now behind the wheel of their truck. Alan and I have contributed a small amount to support a trip to Europe the boys are taking, and they indulged us at dinner as we reminisced (at length) about *our* first trips to Europe as teenagers. Their mother showed us photos of her recent medical mission to Guatemala. I felt connected to this family, to our neighbors, and proud of being connected.

In some way, we are a part of this community. We have roles to play, and we belong. I saw my old boss from the health clinic at the event on Saturday evening, and she asked me out to lunch this week. We had a fraught, competitive relationship in the old days, but now she is retiring, and we both have moved on to different concerns. I look forward to rebuilding that bridge.

The middle way. The way home?

Love,

Chris

April 4, 2023
New York, New York

I FOUND MYSELF WONDERING OVER the white-hot flash of anger in your last letter and hoping you will examine it carefully and thoughtfully, but I also smiled at your tentative embrace of a middle way. Lately, I think that much of how we live can be expressed by the attention we give to the way in which we walk our path. There are times when we are tentative—when moving forward seems too fraught with uncertainty to make the steps anything more than a chore. When I look back at my twenties and thirties, I seem to have skipped and hopscotched my way along heedlessly, not even realizing how many missteps I made or dodged. For now, I feel that I am walking in harmony, as I did years ago when hiking mountain paths in northern Greece—paying attention both to the path and the scenery, alive to the delight of a sudden glimpse of a bird or a darting lizard. I may be more attuned to the present state because it contrasts so starkly with the previous couple of years when I felt as though I were walking in a chain gang, numbly putting one foot in front of the other, moving forward only because failing to move would impact those to whom I was chained. What a numb state of misery. I can recall it, but I no longer feel it.

I also felt a wistfulness at your description of easy intimacy with your person, whether nestling in each other's arms in the warmth of the morning or squabbling happily over the crossword puzzle. The evolution of your relationship, which has been tempered by the cataclysmic news of the past year, reminds me of the process of Damascus steel-making, where the metal is given exceptional beauty, and tensile strength, by being beaten, tested, folded, and heated to the limits of its endurance. (The only reason I know anything about this is that my brother Bill actually forges knives and has made some gorgeous, damascened blades.)

I sometimes wish I had this intimacy in my life. My distant memories of easy mornings curled in bed canoodling with my husband are tinged with sadness over how long ago it really was. Then, I look at my life, my apartment, the sense of self and autonomy and enoughness that I have worked so hard to build, and I am determined not to do anything that could endanger this. I wonder if you could see your perceived loss of independence as a gift that allows you to experience all the love that Alan has to give and to be grateful for your humility in being able to ask for help and his joy in being able to give it. And don't beat yourself up for occasionally being bitchy—the fact that it bothers you means it's out of character, and that you're not some fictional tragic figure who slowly fades whilst clutching her blood-stained handkerchief silently to her chest.

This sort of brings us to that guy who I had been seeing. I like his intelligence, his kindness, his quick humor, his stubborn defense of those who need advocacy despite themselves. However, I don't find him particularly sexy, and he appears to feel the same about me in that he's never done more than give me a hug. We've touched on sensitive subjects, like his sister's death from COVID and my Greg's death, his career changes, the fact that he's never married, and I'm still sort of recovering from my own marriage, but this hasn't sparked any greater intimacy of connection. This lack of connection, combined with my wariness about giving up my autonomy, has led me to decide not to call him again. I feel like I've given it the chance to develop into something, but maintaining a relationship just to have one more person to go out to dinner with seems pointless.

On another topic—religious holidays. You and I have talked about gatherings, specifically about holiday rituals and the warmth and good feeling that comes from sharing traditions much older than ourselves with the people we love.

For me, I have become almost entirely alienated from the "Jesus died for your sins" version of Easter that was the staple of my Catholic childhood. Growing up, we always managed to balance the cognitive dissonance of a week of prayer and liturgical readings centered on suffering, betrayal, and agonizing death with Easter baskets, prettily dyed Easter eggs, new patent leather shoes, and a new Easter dress. The Easter meal, after a morning of triumphant hymns and too much sugar, was always a leg of lamb accompanied by oven-roasted potatoes and mint jelly, served on crisp white linens, all of us dressed in our Sunday best.

I never converted to Greek Orthodoxy—I'm not sure whether I embrace the concept of a deity, but if God exists, I doubt he has an exclusive home team. Nevertheless, I feel much closer to most of the rituals and ceremonies of the Orthodox Church, having baptized my children in that church and having attended some thirty years of Easter services and traditions. Orthodoxy, in general, seems to be much less cruelly aspirational and more human—I wonder if there is a sneaking influence of the old gods, who were famously badly behaved and replete with all the human vices. Most Greeks are reflexively, unthinkingly Orthodox, but it's more a matter of identity than piety. They attend church for weddings, baptisms, and on Easter, which is a far more important holiday than Christmas. Liturgically, this makes sense—the whole point of Christianity, ostensibly, is that God fulfilled his promise of sending the Messiah and granting people access to eternal life, and the evidence of that is the resurrection rather than the birth of the prophet.

The period of Lent is built into the Greek identity, and supermarkets, restaurants, and even coffee shops accommodate the practice of fasting from all animal products with recipes tweaked to be *nistisima* or fasting-compliant. When you and Alan came to Greece for your honeymoon in 2018, I was still running my fast-food franchise business, and you visited one of the shops in Halandri and, I think, tried the freddo espresso—Greece's vastly superior version of iced coffee. During *Sarakosti*, literally "the forty days" of Lent, our shops would offer cheese-free spinach pies, sandwiches with falafel, and plant milk alternatives for coffee.

Holy Week is delineated by ritual preparations for Easter Sunday, which begins at midnight on Saturday night, where the vast majority of the national population can be found in church with their Easter candles. Eggs are boiled on Holy Thursday and dyed red. Friday is the ceremony of the *Epitaphio*, the most mournful liturgy, where a flower-bedecked representation of the tomb is decorated in every parish church and carried through the town (or around Athens) by young men, often accompanied by a brass band playing the beautiful, ancient prayers that are sung in the service. Saturday is spent preparing for the Easter feast. If you're roasting a lamb, as we did often, this means digging the pit, making sure the electric spit-turners work, taking your spit and attendant medieval-looking hardware to your butcher so that he will attach your lamb to its spit, and checking your supplies of charcoal, lemons, butter, and salt because nothing will be open on Easter Sunday if you're running short.

One year, we had ordered our lamb through one rather feckless and perennially broke village neighbor, as a way of helping him make a little money. Unfortunately, he delivered the lamb on Saturday morning and politely but firmly declined to play any part in the very physical and rather grisly task of attaching it to the spit. My husband blew up at me in an unhinged rant in front of our guests because, clearly, this was my fault. The guests and I then scrambled to figure out how to spit a lamb. I remember feeling embarrassed, resentful, and furious at my husband but also perversely proud when we had accomplished the task.

Easter meal prep also means that you peel about twenty-five pounds of potatoes and cut them up for French fries, leaving them to soak overnight in giant tubs of water. Very little is eaten on Holy Saturday, although shellfish is permitted. I've never really understood why lobster and fried calamari were considered fasting-appropriate, but I wasn't about to argue. Ouzo is also permitted . . .

The Easter service begins just before midnight with quiet prayers, the words familiar to all, and the ritual of repeating all things three times to represent the Trinity. Just before midnight, the church lights are turned off, plunging the congregation into darkness. Then the priest appears at the altar holding a single candle and chanting the prayer that begins "*Christos anesti*"—Christ is risen. The congregation responds, "*alithos anesti*"—truly he is risen—and from the one lit candle, all the candles in the church are lit, one by one, as everyone shares the sacred light.

In all my years in Greece, I was only at one Easter service where the small congregation remained to hear the rest of the service. For the most part, once the candles are lit, and we have all sung the "*Christos Anesti*" three times, the congregation beats a hasty retreat, whispered exchanges of the phrases "Christ is risen" and "Truly he is risen"—hugs and kisses punctuating the mass exodus. We all go home to eat *mageiritsa*, the Easter soup made from lamb guts, herbs like dill and fennel, and egg-lemon sauce. It sounds revolting, but I actually enjoyed both making and eating it. (The traditional recipe calls for using the intestines, which I refuse to do. They are just gross and very time-consuming to prepare. I stick with organ meats, cut small and sautéed with red onion.)

The midnight meal focuses on the soup, but the red eggs are also shared and broken in the ritual way—narrow ends ("noses") are bashed together first, and then the battle is repeated for the broad ends ("butts"). A victor is declared, and then the eggs are peeled and eaten. Children vie to have their eggs "win" by staying intact, and many times, a child is slipped a wooden red egg, giggling in delight as their invincible egg takes on all comers.

The meal may run late, but some unlucky soul (this was always me) still has to rise early, pick up the lamb, and probably the *kokoretsi* (more lamb organ meats, wrapped in intestines and absolutely delicious), place the spits, and supervise the burning of the charcoal down to coals. It's a three-to-four-hour process of checking the heat, basting the lamb with the lemon-butter mix, salting, and so on, but it's very social. Everyone in the house ambles out, coffee and *tsoureki* (an Easter bread like challah but soooo much better) in hand, to offer their opinions and company. The wine starts flowing around ten a.m., so both the lamb and the attendants are well-oiled by the time it's ready to eat. Tomatoes, French fries, bread, lemons, and meat—a meal that would look familiar to generations long past, beloved by all. My parents loved to contrast the formal elegance of our childhood Easters with the no-holds-barred, bacchanal spirit of Greek Easter, and while I loved both, I prefer the latter.

My last Easter in Greece was in 2020 during the early, scary part of the pandemic. Everyone was under general lockdown orders, church attendance was forbidden, and the sense of living through a biblical plague was palpable. I cooked a leg of lamb, made French fries and fresh bread, and shared the meal in our Athens garden with Greg and my ex, who managed, true to form, to be churlish and make me regret my generosity in including him. It's been hard to imagine taking part in Easter celebrations since then.

Hope your Passover is wonderful.
Love,
J

April 9, 2023
Breckenridge, Colorado

THE EARTH MOVES. A WEEK ago, Friday, a snow-pocalypse of wind and ice tornadoed around the house. But the next day, the sun appeared, friends arrived, and we celebrated the ritual of Passover.

Now the snow melts in earnest, and a river of water runs beside our dirt road. The robin has returned, and this week, I saw two blue-bird couples examining the bird nesting boxes in our field. I enjoyed a miraculous day of spring skiing—*Me. On skis. One year later.* I received a surprise announcement that my novel has been chosen as a finalist for the Colorado Book Awards.

And somehow, I have been fixated on tablecloths.

I love changing tablecloths with the seasons. What a tablecloth means to me is that I have a place to live with a table, a very nice table. It means that I have a life in which I sit down with my husband to eat meals, in which friends come to visit for dinner. Changing table-cloths signifies an honoring of the progression of the seasons with this little ritual that is smiled upon—not belittled or ignored, or seen as a waste of time or a hassle—by those I love. By folding up one tablecloth, putting it away until next year, and unfolding another to decorate our table, I welcome a movement forward in time, a new season, and my connection to the circle of change and renewal.

I am grateful for these blessings, which were not always a part of my life.

In my early thirties, I was divorced and broke (for the first time) and temporarily moved back in with my parents. Which is why it seems especially ironic that, during this time and while away on a long printing assignment in Verona, Italy, I decided to spend what little money I had on two handmade tablecloths from the Venetian island of Burano. One of the tablecloths was the chaste and classic Burano lace. Lacemaking is a tradition whose origins go back at least to the 1600s, and legend has it that in some enchanted moment of the past, mermaids shared with a few favored local women the gifts of lacemaking and embroidery.

But of these two tablecloths, the one I really love is the second, a large drape of white linen, strewn with bouquets of hand-appliqued flowers and embroidered leaves. A sensual, rippling scalloped edge forms its border. How young I was, with so many experiences still to adventure through, when I decided: *One day, I will have a settled life that calls for beautiful, handmade tablecloths.*

Exactly one year ago yesterday, I had surgery to remove the tumor from the right occipital lobe of my brain. Alan's then eighty-nine-year-old mother and his sister had immediately taken a plane from the East Coast to help us manage once I was released from the hospital. Passover fell on the calendar a few days later. And while Alan's family is Jewish, I was the one who proposed—with a high-pitched steroid-induced insistence—that we celebrate Passover.

Alan's sister and mother shopped for matzo, gefilte fish, and horseradish; they roasted the egg and cooked the matzo ball soup and brisket. Alan baked his stand-out flourless chocolate cake. I wanted to organize the table. After all these years of transporting my tablecloths from one place to the next, I had never actually used the flowered tablecloth from that island off of Venice. After all, it was so, well, *white.* And delicate. It would get spots from food, and one spilled glass of red wine (Passover requires four per person) would spell disaster! I was sure I would never be able to restore it, after its use, to the pristinely smooth, unwrinkled, and unblemished whiteness.

What am I waiting for, I asked myself, at nearly sixty-one years old and recovering from brain surgery? What good, in the end, is "unwrinkled and unblemished whiteness"? And so, I set the table with that never-before-used, hand-embroidered tablecloth. I laid out the gold-rimmed, royal-blue dinner plates I'd inherited from my grandmother that even my mother hesitated to use because the dishes were so over-the-top grandiose. Around each individual setting of dishes, I placed my mother's silver monogrammed knives, forks, and spoons.

We stumbled through the words of the Haggadah with Alan and his sister trying to recall their relaxed childhood Hebrew language training; Alan's feisty, opinionated mother announced several times her disbelief in God, then as if in explanation, recounted her history as a labor organizer in the 1940s. One of my close friends was the Passover guest, gamely taking helpings of the scary gefilte fish and the horseradish. I was inspired and overwhelmed by the sense that death had, at least for now, passed over me. I felt washed over with blessings that we were together, all of us imperfect humans.

Glasses of red wine were spilled on my white tablecloth. With a rubbing of salt and an overnight soak in warm water, the tablecloth rinsed clean.

We celebrated Passover again this year with friends. This time, Alan read from a Haggadah he had adapted himself, leaving in (for my sake, so he said) gratitude to God. The food, wine, and Alan's reading wove a kind of spell around us, empowering each person to share something of loss and suffering, of compassion and hope for the rebirth and renewal promised by spring. Once again, the Passover ritual filled me with gratitude at having made it through the Narrow Straits of illness.

Back in November, I wrote an entry about trying to make peace with my father's reaction to an old photograph. Today, I think I understand his unexpected display of emotion a little bit better. Yesterday, Alan and I attended a seminar presented by the neurosurgery department at the university hospital and had a chance to talk to the chairman, Dr. Kevin Lillehei, who performed my brain surgery. I had brought a signed copy of my novel for him; a year ago to the day, his quick action on my behalf, rushing me into surgery, not only saved my life but allowed me to finish and see the publication of this book that has meant so much to me. He teared up, gave me a big hug, and said he thought he was going to cry.

Perhaps, in that moment between us, my surgeon held both the knowledge that even with his skill, his years of experience, and his best intentions, surgeries don't always turn out successfully—as well as a humbling gratitude that, in the case of my operation, he had succeeded in fulfilling the task to which he had committed his life.

I wonder now if the photo I showed my father so many years ago, holding my hand and my sister's as we skipped down a dirt road, reminded him of his own successes and failures in his relationships with his children—those in his care.

Around the time that photo was taken, my father had lost both his parents in a violent accident. Back then, he'd been a young lawyer just starting out in his father's firm. His good character and emotionally controlled upbringing would never have permitted him, with a wife and three young children depending upon him, to break down and give in to grief. Though he never faltered in his role as husband, father, and provider, to my sorrow and confusion as a child, the playful, attentive father I knew disappeared. For many years, my father withdrew into work or long-distance running; occasionally, he became violently angry.

When I surprised him with that photo so many years later, I can now imagine some of what may have caused his tears: The memory of his parents' sudden death, uncertainty and regret over how his grief may have affected him as a father and a husband. I understand now the weight a person of commitment and good intentions can feel toward their responsibility: *Did I do all I could? Was it enough?*

Now, a week after Passover and in celebration of Easter, I have washed and pressed my Burano tablecloth. I've replaced it with another cloth, one I received from my grandmother, an unbleached linen, good for everyday use.

I don't want to ignore your observation (or my mother-in-law's!) that religious holidays can stir up conflict, disagreement, or painful associations. So, I'll finish by saying that the tablecloth I lay down today, decorated with wreaths of flowers, represents my simple and ongoing commitment to the celebration of springtime and to my faith in the possibility of growth and renewal.

Love,
Chris

April 11, 2023
New York, New York

I LOVED YOUR LAST LETTER for the conscious awareness of blessings, the evolving reverence for symbols, the humor of dealing with families, and the epiphany—I think I can call it that—about your father's complicated response to the crushing weight of love.

For you, the Passover seder has become a new way to celebrate continuity, survival, gratitude, and, of course, industrial quantities of brisket. Even in the way the brisket is prepared, with days of marinating and a long, slow cooking process, there is a mindful wisdom to the rituals that add meaning. The fact that Alan has adapted the Haggadah to your particular circumstances demonstrates that religions live and thrive if their rituals and prayers also adapt to the changing circumstances, bending but not breaking.

Tablecloths. For most of the thirty years I lived in Greece, customs were still formal, and my ex was adamant that we be equipped to set a formal table. As a result, at least when it came to entertaining, we led a tablecloth life, embracing the signifiers of elegant living prevalent among our peers. We had my mother's splendid Rosenthal china, a service for twelve, rimmed in 24-karat gold, with only a couple of teacups missing. (My parents had acquired this set in Germany in 1962 for a song, one of the benefits of being stationed in France in the post-WWII years. My mother passed it on to me after we married, reasoning that we would use them more than they would now that the occasions on which my parents were planning to set a formal table were few and far between.) We registered for a Christofle silver service and Baccarat wine and water goblets, and filled out our set with wedding gifts and a few judicious purchases. Our Wellesley classmate Mercedes was one of my bridesmaids, and her parents gave us a wedding gift of a spectacular Spanish linen tablecloth and napkins for twelve—gossamer-thin and adorned with lace cut-outs. I had a few other tablecloths for smaller dinners, but the Benavides tablecloth saw service on multiple occasions, despite the fact that ironing it was a full-day operation. In those days, I had a live-in housekeeper and resigned myself to much ostentatious sighing and exhaling as she wrestled with its diabolical capacity for wrinkling.

As my ex climbed the corporate ladder to president of his bank, our dinner salons were both frequent and formal. I resisted his call to have more than ten guests, which would have required a second table since, for me, if you've invited people to dinner, you should share the damn table with them. I did the meal planning, food shopping, and most of the cooking, even though we often had someone to finish the dishes and serve. For the fanciest evenings, we had our housekeeper and a cook in the kitchen and a tuxedoed waiter serving drinks from a silver salver and then hovering with the laden tray at the dining room table, serving from the left and clearing from the right. Long evenings, since dinner in Greece doesn't begin before ten in the evening. I took pride in the compliments, even though I was much happier eating in the family room with the boys, and loathed waking up at half past six in the morning to make breakfast and get the boys out the door after having gone to bed at two in the morning.

We also had a tablecloth on our everyday family room table, which was a rough farm table with a functional but unlovely top. These were smaller, more colorful and durable cloths of cotton, very forgiving of spilled milk and tomato sauce. My mother had made two of these, and others were acquired over the years; they had all grown thin with love and wear.

When I returned to Greece in the fall of 2021 to choose what I would take back to the US, I deliberated carefully over which items would make the very short list of things I wanted to keep. I chose two small, packable carpets, each of which represented a warm memory with the man whom I had once loved. I rescued my mother's china, which she then consigned to a sale to benefit her local charity. I had no interest in the carefully curated crystal and silver, the fish forks and serving pieces, all the signifiers of a life that I had once lived. I kept my sons' baby spoons and a handful of silver pieces that I loved and left the rest to my flabbergasted ex, who I think had expected me to haggle over them. I will confess that, in a moment of vengefulness, I methodically smashed a set of rather lovely green crystal glasses to bits with a hammer—they had been a gift from the woman who I thought was my friend and belatedly came to recognize was my husband's longtime lover. I do not regret that at all. I don't think he even missed them, but if he did, he hasn't dared to ask about them.

I left almost all my tablecloths behind, including that legendary Spanish linen-and-lace concoction. Mercedes had died of cervical cancer ten days after Greg, and the life that I had lived was now as ill-fitting as an outgrown coat. I kept my mother's soft Irish linen cloth, a delectable mint-pistachio shade of green, and one of the simple, everyday cloths that I had leaned my elbows on with my boys over so many meals. Neither of these fits any table that I now own or am likely to own, but they are important to me nonetheless.

I confess I felt a stab to my heart when I read about your encounter with your surgeon—I recognize that feeling of joy inextricably commingled with the fear of not living up to the responsibility to the beings I had created. I can bring to mind, instantly, the rush of fierce love I felt looking on my sleeping babies' faces; I would have killed to protect them, with no hesitation. Each time they stumbled, or were hurt by something I couldn't fix, it was an almost physical pain. When Greg was bullied in middle school, I felt a homicidal rage at the wretched diplomat's brat who was his chief tormentor, matched with an awful sense of helplessness. And yes, while I know that I did everything in my power to nurture him, to protect him, to give him wings and a sense of his potential, ultimately, I failed to protect him. This is not rational, I know, but neither is love.

Early on, I told you the story of one of my last conversations with my father when he wanted me to know the story of one of his last surgeries. He rarely talked about his daily experiences, but when I was about twelve, I remember a day when he had come home from the hospital profoundly shaken and gathered his children to give us an out-of-character stern lecture about the danger of fire. It turns out that he had spent much of his afternoon inserting tracheostomies in the throats of two young boys who had accidentally set themselves on fire playing with matches. I can remember his steady voice shaking as he described their blackened bodies and the desperate efforts of an entire emergency room to give them a chance of survival; they both died within the week. A good surgeon, like a good father, is proud of the successes and haunted by the failures, even if the failure was in no way within their ability to control. I guess it's the curse of caring; without love, though, what, really, is the point?

Today, I spent three very satisfying hours in the park removing mugwort. *Artemisia vulgaris* is endemic to Europe and is regarded a useful folk remedy as a tisane. It seems to have been introduced to North America by Jesuits in the sixteenth century; it's notoriously difficult to eliminate, an exuberant and wily thug of a plant that crowds out endemic species, so weeding it is an exercise in optimism and persistence.

Mugwort removal provides a socially accepted context for stabbing things with a large utility knife, something I needed this week. My wasband had angered me with a grand gesture that, to me, felt like an attention-grabbing stunt. He serves on the board of a shipping company owned by friends, and they recently christened a newly built, state-of-the-art container ship *Gregos*. There was an elaborate ceremony in Korea at the shipyard where it was built; my ex had invited Yannis and me, and I was happy to have my new job as an excuse for not attending. It took a lot of self-control and gritting of teeth to listen to Yannis's anger without fueling it, and while I think I did a good job of presenting a Swiss-level neutrality, I had great motivation to stab things with gusto and intention. I was once again very grateful for the grounding connection with the dirt, the reward of seeing the tiny, shy, bright green perennials poke through the soil once the shading invader was dislodged. What a wonderful, painful, extraordinary thing is a life.

Love,

J

April 13, 2023
Breckenridge, Colorado

W E DROVE TO THE HISTORIC hot springs in Glenwood, Colorado, with Alan's sister and her husband, who are visiting. As we wound through shadowy Glenwood Canyon, the Colorado River running high and fast below us, my mind kept returning to the bright descriptions in your letter of the formal dinners you and your husband presided over. I imagined the glinting silver, gold-rimmed plates, sparkling crystal, the waiters. And you, a Henry James heroine! A young American woman, Greek wife, and the hostess to such splendid evenings.

In the middle of the night, I awoke in our room at the Hotel Colorado, overcome with shame and remorse. I'd had a dream of us as students at Wellesley, our futures aglow *with so much promise.* Why, the young married life you described was exactly the promising outcome my parents would have wanted for me!

Your own parents must have been so proud: You had managed to combine adventure with a seemingly comfortable marriage in a gorgeous setting, a glittering social life, financial security, and a family. I understand this is a vast oversimplification—perhaps mostly tortured fantasy on my part—but your description does, indeed, suggest that you skipped and hopscotched gracefully through this period of your life.

Meanwhile, on the other side of the Atlantic and at about the same moment, I was living in an un-air-conditioned, fifth-floor studio walk-up in Manhattan with a man I had married despite knowing in advance that he was abusive and an alcoholic. Pretty sure that I would have to support him on my meager publishing salary until the much-talked-about day when he "sold his next novel."

My first husband was charismatic, the author of two published novels, and his parents were the literary agents for a number of intellectuals and poets. Stepping foot for the first time in this world of urban intellectuals thrilled me: the martinis at Bemelmans bar at the Carlyle, late-night winter taxi rides to Rumplemeyer's on Central Park South for hot chocolate, the passionate conversations that often devolved into dramatic and sometimes physical arguments, the casual references to well-known writers and artists who were apparently family friends.

My parents and grandparents abhorred this man and his family, who were equally disdainful of my family—seeing them as smug and suburban. Ironically, perhaps my parents' complete incomprehension and horror were at least part of what seduced me.

And what came to mind as I lay in bed two nights ago and relived the awful degradation and abuse to which this period of my life descended—a life I had chosen!—was a particular scene of this man and me drinking ourselves into oblivion on the roof of our Manhattan brownstone. We drank Roederer Cristal champagne from a set of six Waterford crystal goblets we had received from friends of his parents after we'd decided (in another drunken moment) to take a cab to city hall and get married. After downing each full goblet of champagne, we threw our glasses off the rooftop, laughing uproariously as they smashed five floors down in the courtyard below. Among so many other questions, why hadn't it occurred to either of us that we could have hit and injured someone?

If this young woman had been a character in a story, today I would probably shake my head, I might shudder—or I might even laugh. But this was me, reveling in destruction and self-destruction. It is no wonder, I thought, slinking deeper under the covers in my hotel bed, that the Gods of Fine Tablecloths had chosen to withhold from me, until my fifties, a life of dining among nice things. Perhaps, I imagined, they'd judged ten years would suffice for each of the three Waterford crystal goblets I had carelessly smashed. Now tossing and turning, I kept asking myself: *How could I have done this?* So violently turned my back on seeking a better, more wholesome kind of life? I finally fell asleep, and when I awoke, felt drugged with self-loathing.

Very Calvinistic, as you would likely point out.

At breakfast the next morning, while the rest of our foursome bossed the waiter around like the New Yorkers we all are, requesting exceptions to each entrée ordered from the menu, I slumped in my seat. Then, I noticed music being piped into the dining room, a soundtrack from the 1970s and '80s. Some of the songs came back to me from our high school days—not the names, which eluded me, but the tunes themselves and how they had made me feel. Songs of love, of the road, songs of moving on. Songs that had filled me with an irrepressible desire to get in the car, or on a train or airplane and *just go.*

Then another aspect of the years of domestic chaos resurfaced in my mind. In my twenties, I had fallen into a weird subset of publishing, managing the color printing of art books, which required me to travel around the world many months out of the year. I wish I could have felt differently, but the truth is it *suited me* to have one husband, and then a second, who I felt justified in leaving behind; it *suited me* to be alone to experience the incredible exuberance and sense of being transformed and fully alive as I touched down in each new place: Zurich, Milan, Bangkok, Tokyo, and breathtakingly glamorous Hong Kong.

This line of work was so niche and particular. To my delight, my talent for it made me sought after by museums and art book publishers. And I see now I could not have given up the experience of moving through each of those different worlds, a changed version of myself, absorbing every detail of landscape, food, clothing, artwork, music, and unlikely friendships on my own solitary terms.

I think back to what I wrote a few days ago about a wish that I had as a young woman to one day live a life that called for beautiful tablecloths. A way of understanding this is to see that it wasn't a desire that a settled life would somehow find me. It was more that, deep inside, the young woman who I was hoped that the day would come when I would stop feeling so restless and unmoored and stop getting into relationships that could only end in violent break-ups. But I wasn't quite ready. There is that saying attributed to Saint Augustine: "Give me chastity and continence, *but not yet.*"

Once, I hoped I would want a life of calm and beauty and the peace of having someone to share it with. At sixty-one, I must try to accept that while I wished I could have been that person in my twenties and thirties or even forties, I wasn't her just yet. And today, I try to expand my understanding and compassion to the young woman I was: so docile and angelic-looking in photos and who so often just wanted to break things.

It's funny, isn't it, that having followed such different paths you and I have both come to this point in life with just a few material things that really matter to us. Which include one or two tablecloths.

I wanted to share these words, all that I can remember, from a dream I had a few days later:

> Hands no longer
> clenched in fists
> but cupped to
> receive blessings

Love,
Chris

April 24, 2023
New York, New York

Y OU HAVE FOUND A PATH of grace in receiving, in cupping your hands to accept blessings. It was a lesson I learned after Greg died, when I didn't have the strength to put on a brave face and hide behind my usual competent, dispassionate, deflect-emotion-with-humor shield. I was too exhausted to hide my vulnerability and thus accidentally discovered the grace of accepting the love and blessings that good people were offering me. I've been trying to do the same for others, but it's a wonderful gift, isn't it?

In that spirit of kindness and humility, try not to be too hard on the young Christina, who lived close to the edge and hurled crystal off rooftops. It's part of the journey of becoming who you've become, and if it were anyone else describing the more eye-popping moments of their misspent youth, you'd respond with humor, kindness, and understanding. You deserve at least the same.

I also want to express my renewed admiration for all those women who wrote after their kids had gone to bed, early in the morning before they went to work after everyone else demanding their attention and time had gone to sleep. What hunger to be heard they must have had!

Over the years of raising the boys and making a life in Greece, I would on rare occasions take the time to sit down and record my impressions, but I wish I had done more of it, and consistently. At least now we are writing, even though I feel guilty that I couldn't carve out time to write while I had guests for a week.

On the subject of guests . . .

My friend Valeria and her nearly fifteen-year-old son, Alexandros, stayed with me again this year for a week. Last year, my apartment was still a shambolic work in progress. I had very little furniture and had to borrow towels and an inflatable mattress from my son, and I wasn't working or even volunteering steadily, so we had a lot of time to be tourists. I was struck then by their hesitance to do anything without me—Manhattan is a grid, they had a US phone card with unlimited access to data, including Google maps, so I found it baffling, but so be it.

Valeria has been my dear friend for over thirty years. I've seen her through her second marriage and its dissolution, the birth and tragic loss of her firstborn child to a rare and virulent cancer at age four, her third marriage and its dissolution, and her transformation from former runway model to psychologist and family counselor. The day after Greg's funeral in Athens, Yannis returned to New York, and I, broken, broken-hearted, and so afraid for him, resolved to get there as soon as possible, moved to Valeria's house, where she and her housekeeper basically wrapped me in cotton wool, fed me, held me, and kept me somewhat whole until I got on the plane. I stay with her, for weeks and even months at a time, any time I am in Greece. (Her housekeeper, Irina, is a warm, unintentionally hilarious, fiercely loyal, and hot-tempered Moldavian who I can only describe as a hybrid drill sergeant/Mary Poppins. Irina has a tiny parakeet, named Achilles because one of his feet is injured, who at eighteen has lived far beyond the usual parakeet lifespan and murmurs affirmations to himself in Russian all day.) Valeria is on the top of the list of friends who I could call at two in the morning, say "I need your help," and she would ask, calmly, if I needed a tarp, a shovel, or an alibi.

So, it goes without saying that Valeria is welcome at any time, even though I take up much less space in her enormous home than she and her son do in my one-bedroom Manhattan apartment. Alexandros is at that teenage phase where he communicates in grunts and is possessed of the magical ability to become an invertebrate and languidly spill over any horizontal surface at will. Very little other than basketball interests him, and his food preferences are limited to sugar in many forms and Shake Shack burgers. I adore this boy, as I have since he was born, but this is still a hard age to love, and his mother is disinclined to crack the whip and insist that he move with more alacrity and enthusiasm than an expiring Victorian consumptive. Not my kid, and given her history of loss and what we've been through together, I am not going to interfere, but my patience was tested over the course of the week.

I also realized that she and I have different insecurities and occasionally, and unintentionally, trigger each other. She is no longer the eighteen-year-old who shared a runway with Cindy Crawford and Iman, but she still gets mistaken for Julia Roberts and is impossibly beautiful and effortlessly stylish. I am pleasant enough looking, but my body was designed by Lego, and my fashion sense can be described as "there appears to have been a struggle." Most of the time, I'm completely content with this genetic roll of the dice and am actually grateful that I never tied my self-worth to my appearance. I've consistently identified as being smart, funny, and kind, and I'm happy with this. But I still look at the photos of us together and can feel twinges of insecurity. Conversely, I read incessantly and widely and have a magpie brain that retains a great deal of information, and I think I can be intimidating when Valeria, who began her academic studies in her late forties and who has worked very hard at acquiring her master's in psychology, mentions some tidbit of information only to discover that I (a) have an opinion and (b) may have read more than she has on the subject. So, I have resolved to recognize and forgive my own insecurities and to be a bit more sensitive about provoking hers.

I had other encounters during the week of their visit, both in person and over the internet, which added to my experiences in ways that I'm still processing. The day before their arrival, I met one of my *koumbaras* for coffee. *Koumbara* is the Greek term for a relationship that is created by a familial obligation—either the person has stood for you at your wedding, or has baptized your child, or you have baptized theirs. In Ninetta's case, our relationship is knitted together at multiple levels. Her husband has been one of my ex's closest friends since they were eight years old, and he was a groomsman at our wedding, my ex was a groomsman at theirs, I am the godmother to their son and she is (was?) my son Greg's godmother, so our blood-bond is practically incestuous. We're very different in many ways—she's much more of a classic Greek mother than I ever was—but we are also bound together, formally and through friendship. She and her husband searched for Greg the night he took his life; they came to the airport to pick me and Yannis up and take us to the morgue to see him. Her love for Greg was simple, unwavering, and warm, and he loved her deeply.

About a year ago, we had a falling out. She revealed in a casual phone conversation that she had been discussing Greg with friends at a cocktail party and had learned that there was security camera footage of him spending several hours pacing the Niarchos Center, working up the courage to go to the top and leap. To me, it felt incredibly callous both that she was discussing Greg's death at a party and that she didn't consider that off-handedly reporting details of his final hours would unleash in me a wounding spiral of guilt and grief. I stopped talking to her; I didn't communicate with her when I was in Greece last summer, and while I texted her to get together for coffee when I went in November, I wasn't all that sorry when our schedules didn't work out. I missed our friendship, but it felt permanently damaged.

So, when Ninetta texted me that she would be in NYC for a month, visiting her daughter, it was a chance to clear the air. Neither of us danced around it—she knew why I was so upset, but wanted to give me the context, and I was distant enough from the initial hurt that I could explain why it was so wounding without shutting down. We truly heard each other, acknowledged both the insensitivity and my reaction (over-reaction?) to it, and we're back on terms of trust and affection, which feels healing. We later met with our kids for brunch, and it was lovely to see them together, friends from childhood, each making their way as young professionals in New York. Resolutions are things to be grateful for.

The other profound encounter of my week was an indirect one with the writer Neil Gaiman[1] as part of a lecture series at Bard College. The theme of the series was what it means to be a bard, and it was an entrancing hour and half of wit, philosophy, literary analysis, and just profound hopefulness about the health of the human imagination.

Gaiman identified two bard prototypes—the Beowulf, who is the Homeric itinerant performer who needs to capture the imagination of his audience in order to be fed, or, in the case of Scheherazade, to avoid being killed. There are formulaic phrases; there are deliberate repetitions; there are recognizable patterns; and there are what Gaiman describes as "good lies that tell true things." The other prototype is Dante, the creator who has managed to find a wealthy and trusting patron who gives them the security to create stories and lessons, that may be riskier, less comfortable, less predictable but equally captivating.

To Gaiman, the fundamental question in any storytelling environment is "And then, what happened?" Humans are curious, we want to know the resolution, we want to be piqued to continue the story, and we are comforted by perceiving the lesson of the moment even as we want the adventure to continue.

---

[1] It would be disingenuous to ignore the horrifying allegations that have recently come to light with respect to this writer. However, it would feel dishonest to ignore the power of his storytelling even as it complicates how I feel about that influence. ~Jane

Another phrase he used, that struck me so deeply that I wrote it down, as though I were attending a college lecture for credit, was a general reflection on telling stories: "We save our lives in such unlikely ways."

I submit that this writing exchange, this epistolary conversation, fits neither the Beowulf nor the Dante paradigm of the storyteller, but is also an example of an unlikely way in which we can save our lives. I'm so grateful for our conversation.

J

May 1, 2023
Saint John, USVI

OUR STUDIO IS A KIND of crow's nest with a wraparound deck on the East End above Privateer Bay. How happy I am to be back in Saint John, listening to the rolling in of waves over the stony beach, the squawk and tweet of birds, the b-a-a-a-a-a-h! of goats. But mostly silence, with the sounds like brush strokes of color against a canvas of deep quiet and serenity.

In your letter, you described two long-time relationships of yours. I was drawn in by imagining the person you were many years ago as these friendships began and developed, and who you are now when so much has changed—reaching inside yourself for patience, understanding, and the possibility of forgiveness. Recognizing the connection you have with these old friends, accepting the love these people have for you (and you for them) along with their more annoying qualities of self-involvement, lack of initiative, and uninspired palates tending toward Shake Shack! I envied you the lecture you described with Neil Gaiman! I loved the ways he characterized storytelling. With this writing, I think I do feel a little like Scheherazade . . .

On this trip to Saint John, I brought a book called *Reconciliation* by Thich Nhat Hanh. In the case of this book, the theme is cultivating love and acceptance toward one's self as a child. I've been thinking about the harsh and often unforgiving perspective I hold towards my younger self, which you've noticed too. The "Why did I do this? Why did I do that? What was wrong with me?" *What* was *wrong with me?*

These days and especially at home in our usual surroundings, that inclination to blame myself—to find that younger self shameful—somehow gets tangled up with the tremendous fear that overtakes me at times related to my health. It's odd how I write: "related to." The thing is, I can't tell for sure what, exactly, I am afraid of. Is it death (it's gotta be), long weeks of suffering (and for sure that), but even so . . . It seems like something else too. The closest I can get to describing it is a fear of being cast out. Everyone I love, everything I care about on one side. And me, ejected into some dark, cold space where I am all alone.

The other night, as I started *Reconciliation*, I followed the instructions, to an exercise: turn my attention away from all the many usual distractions and listen for the voice of the child inside. Invite this child into your presence, embrace her. "In the past, I left you alone. I went away from you. Now, I am very sorry. I am going to embrace you." Thinking this gave me a warm, kindly feeling, and I fell asleep.

The next morning, I awoke with a vivid memory of being twelve years old, banished (in my view at the time) to a monthlong, sleep-away tennis clinic I had vigorously protested attending. I wanted to spend the New Hampshire summer as I always had: just a kid waking up to mostly unstructured days of swimming, drawing, playing with the dog, hiking, and going out for ice cream with my brother and sister. I had zero interest in tennis, but it was a prestigious camp and, in our circle, tennis was considered (by my parents and grandparents—none of whom played tennis) to be a useful social skill.

Four days in, I got my period for the first time.

For two years, since first learning about menstruation in fifth grade, I had lived in dread of this moment. In fact, I realized upon waking from this dream the other morning that I'd anticipated my period with the same fear that I now anticipate illness, death. The end of everything that was meaningful to me and most particularly my life as a physically free and unencumbered being.

With the commencement of my period, my life would now consist of always waiting to feel ill and to bleed, to be swaddled in bulky padding. To have people feel sorry for me, and me making excuses for why I was tired, had to lie down, or couldn't do certain things. There would be no more swimming—the thing I loved the most— without fear of "What if my period starts right now?" I had heard girls say that they stopped activities altogether and just went to bed for ten days.

When I emerged from the bathroom that morning at camp, having stuffed my underwear with a wad of toilet paper to keep the frightening brown ooze of blood from staining my tennis whites, I knew my life was over.

The female counselors dropped their usual teasing and slightly superior banter and were immediately kind. We went to the store in town to buy supplies, and they sat me down to explain how all of this was normal, then showed me how to rig up the horrid belt and pad. (Did these female counselors do this too? That was hard to believe.) I remember being given space, time to myself, in which I went to bed for two days more from existential despair than pain.

Eventually, the cramps and bleeding subsided. Shaken and humiliated, I pulled myself together and got dressed. I marched into the counselors' lounge and announced I would no longer take tennis classes. I'd never wanted to learn tennis, so now I put my foot down. From that day forward, I spent my time reading, hiking in the woods, and searching for snakes. No one objected. Looking back, I admire my firmness and determination.

About two-thirds of the way through the month, one of the women counselors—Laurie, who had helped me with the menstrual pads and belts—woke all the older girls up in the middle of the night.

The camp, she explained in a whisper, had a tradition of "midnight skinny dipping" with older girls sneaking out on one night to swim and older boys on another night.

I wanted to go; I loved swimming. But my body had become untrustworthy. What if I got my period again in the middle of the swim? But I understood it was an honor to be invited, while the younger kids stayed back in their bunks. I clambered out of my bed and joined the group.

We ran down the unlit road to an old bridge. Beneath the bridge lay a deep, frigidly cold pool. All us girls stumbled and slid down off the road, away from possible car headlights—unlikely on this country road. More likely and surprisingly thrilling was the idea of boys. We climbed up onto the boulders surrounding the black surface of the pool. And there we stood, looking into the mysterious water.

Suddenly, Laurie peeled off all her clothes. In the dark, she was very pale and stood calmly on a rock beside the pool. She looked at it, judging. And then she dove in. Another girl pulled off her clothes, and then another. All very purposefully and without any sense of embarrassment. And perhaps as a way to recapture some of my lost dignity, I was one of those first girls.

The water was so black, and the space undefined, disorienting. The cold shock of it! I surfaced, gasping, different but better. I had accepted this burden; I could handle it. I was part of this group of pale-limbed night swimmers unafraid to dive blindly into the frigid, enigmatic waters. Tennis camp disappeared, supplanted by a more primordial ritual place of transformation.

I began this letter writing about the efforts of my adult self to reconcile with the child I once was. But now it seems to me that my childhood self has kindly reached out to the adult me. Could she be reminding me that, once, a long time ago, I experienced a similar existential terror of abandonment and the loss of my self? I see, now, that even at that young age, I was resilient, able to assert myself and find new connections, capable of staring down fear, and curious about the unknown.

Will there be a dark pool of transformation down the road for me? Before which I, as others have before me, strip down, dive in, and emerge transformed, having accepted what could not be changed?

The ocean down below me flings its waves roughly on the rocky beach. According to Buddhist thought, we are connected not only to people such as ancestors before us, children who will come after us, and younger and older versions of ourselves, but also to all things. Within our cells are the tiny fragments of all of life that has come before: rocks, trees, animals, the ocean.

When I walk down to stand before the ocean, I listen to the crash and hiss of waves in front of me, and then the subsequent crashes one after the next further down the beach. Underneath it all is a rumbling, a booming sound. I don't think it is thunder, it sounds as if it is coming from somewhere deep below the water, or from inside the cliffs, or from within the air itself.

Love,
Chris

May 5, 2023
New York, New York

IT WAS YOUR BIRTHDAY THIS week. I thought of you, of course, sent my wishes, and wondered about how it was to celebrate it. Your sixtieth was likely an unmitigated celebration, a milestone in a solid life filled with experiences, anticipation, companionship, and finally, a life companion worthy of the name. Then, your sixty-first, when all was in chaos, when you were still reeling from surgery, diagnosis, the inescapable reality of a close dependence on doctors, hospitals, pharmaceutical regimens, all the things that had been outside your realm of experience. So, what was sixty-two? Where did the maelstrom of feeling settle? Anger and fear, still, I assume, but also gratitude, a sense of empowerment, the ability to look up at the sword of Damocles over your head with something like equanimity. I don't know.

But I contrasted your story of the moment of diving into the dark pool of transformation with a story you shared with me, before your diagnosis, about swimming lessons at Wellesley. I find I am seeing a transformed Chris. It's as though you've chosen, consciously, to find the magic and the power in experiences rather than to ruminate on the times when you felt less significant, more awkward, more vulnerable in naked exposure. I wish that for you. One of the "truisms" I read after Greg died, which is still gradually sinking in, is that the only control we have over events is how we react to them. In the beginning, I didn't think I had the mental vocabulary to absorb what this meant. But as I sat last week, talking over lunch with a friend from Turkey, who was visiting her daughters who live in NYC, I realized that I meant it when I told her that I am no longer afraid of things. What can life do to me that I cannot face? It's a sort of WTF equanimity, but it's still a strength.

I was back weeding mugwort this week, but the tactics had changed. The lovely young man who manages the team of volunteers does a brilliant job of guiding without chiding, trying to make sure that we (literally) tread lightly over the naturalized slope while explaining why, at this stage of development, mugwort requires mitigation but is no longer susceptible to eradication. When everything is tiny, we try to dig out the roots and eliminate them. But as the plants grow, and their roots entangle and cross, it's like throwing out the baby with the bathwater to go slicing into the soil with the pruning knives, so we are encouraged to pull what's above ground, hoping to get the roots but content with impeding the plants' access to nutrients and sunlight by stripping the foliage.

I discovered that this particular hunt required a frequent shift of perspective—crouched on my haunches or bent from the waist, every shift of my feet a sort of Twister exercise of hitting a bald spot where I won't crush some emerging plant, I happily and methodically worked through one satisfyingly large patch, threading my gloved hands through the shy variegated violets and other endemics to pluck the offending mugwort. Nose close to the ground, I smiled in satisfaction at the newly freed patch, the light and air I bestowed, like a minor benevolent deity, on the native plants. Then, standing and stretching the kinks out of my back, which reminded me that flexibility is a gift of the young, I would look from a height at the area one meter beyond my now tiny clear spot into a veritable forest of eight-inch-high mugwort plants. *Sigh.* And on to the next. It made me think of how much we can see with even minor shifts in perspective, and how important it is to engage ourselves with kindness and humor.

As I weeded, my mind (which, as you know, is run by an unruly pack of squirrels or maybe ferrets) went off in various directions, including favorite words in Greek. Many, possibly most, Greeks will name *iliovasilema* ("sunset") or *thalassa* ("sea"), both for the poetry of their sound and for the images and sounds that they evoke. I think my favorite is the rather weird word *agalliasi*, accented on the first *i*. It means something like exalted joy—I think the closest expression I can come up with that matches the frisson of happiness, peace, and integral joy that this word evokes for me is from Mary Oliver's poem "Mindful": Something that more or less kills me with delight.

I used to experience this when walking, just after dawn or at sunset, on the beach in Agiannaki, where I was alone with the shore, the iodine smell of the sea, the gentle susurrus of the waves, the wheeling seabirds, and the changing light on the pebbles just at the edge of the sand. For the first two years after Greg's death, I was either leaden or slashed with grief, and the feeling seemed both unreal and unattainable, like drinking wine from Mars or learning to fly. Lately, I have had flashes of this again, and it's all the more wonderful because I believed it cauterized at the nub.

So, my birthday wish for you is moments of *agalliasi*, where you experience the rare and unexpected sense of total integrity in the moment, of joy that defies analysis, of happiness to be alive in that second and to require nothing more.

> Happiest of birthdays, my dear friend,
> J

May 12, 2023
Saint John, USVI

WITH A PSYCHEDELIC DISPLAY OF light and color, the sun blazed behind clouds before slipping into the ocean as Alan and I celebrated at Zozo's in Caneel Bay. Thank you for the birthday wishes! I ordered a big, ice-cold martini, one of my favorite indulgences (from the bad old days), and for a few blissful hours, I stopped asking myself, *Will this be my last birthday?*

We seem to have a Mary Oliver thread running through our letters, so I'll start with this: Like so many people, I'll wager, I was introduced to Mary Oliver with the lines from "The Summer Day": "Tell me, what is it you plan to do / with your one wild and precious life?" And they provoked an urgency to question whether I was truly making the most of my "one wild and precious life." I read those lines and vowed to find and savor the feeling of being blessed, of experiencing joy.

What I have been struggling with these past weeks here in Saint John is that the anticipation of dying (maybe sooner, maybe later) is also a good excuse to turn away from joy: After all, what is the point? Your heart just breaks harder at all you are losing.

I have been plodding through Thich Nhat Hanh's *Reconciliation*. In a certain way, I feel as if I am beating my head against a wall as I attempt to repeat, over and over again: "I breathe in and welcome myself as a child; I breathe out and smile at myself as a child." And multiple variations on this theme. What a surprise that the path to enlightenment is not a quick and easy jaunt to pick up a few things you forgot at the grocery store.

A few days ago, we were at one of our favorite beaches, Frances Bay. It has soft white sand for relaxing, lovely turquoise water for swimming, and fantastic underwater areas of sea grass and coral for snorkeling. Alan had swum out immediately, hoping to meet up with a barracuda or moray eel; doggedly, I was struggling through the practice of Tonglen, "breathing in fear, breathing out acceptance," and so on. Inviting my inner child to join me in what felt like a very mournful exercise.

Some kind of fussing had been going on in the background and now reached a pitch of wailing I could not ignore. I looked up. A young mother was speaking very reasonably to her red-faced and recalcitrant child: "Don't you want to share your goggles with Jimmy?"

"Nooooooooo!"

I put down my book and watched this little kid, who I could tell was just pissed off at more or less everything. He did not want to share; he did not want to play with Jimmy or let Jimmy borrow his goggles. And as it turned out, when his mother said it was now time to go home, he dug into the sand with a shovel and ignored her completely. He did not want to go home, either!

I found myself completely enthralled with this exchange, and rooting for this kid. Nothing was going to make him happy. *Yup*, I completely get that. Eventually, he walked to the shore and scowled at the impassive ocean.

"We had fun today, didn't we?" his mother cajoled.

"No," he pronounced, and let his mother pick him up.

Was I once like this as a child? This is not how I remember myself, and yet . . . he did remind me an awful lot of a twelve-year-old girl who refused to play tennis. Possibly, at this moment, the universe had decided to introduce to me some version of my inner child, a young boy with whom I felt complete solidarity and connection. Gratitude made me smile; how amazing to receive what I had asked for, but did not expect to welcome in exactly this packaging. This was a stubborn kid who needed to do things his own way, to resist nice and reasonable suggestions (*Fuck sharing! Screw Jimmy!*), to resist being happy even. After all, why not devote oneself to the task of determinedly digging a hole in the sand to China? Beginning here on the beach in Saint John.

Two days later, Alan and I went for a hike in the hills above Cinnamon Bay. The crumbling stone walls of an old sugar factory rest in a shady grove of bay rum trees. These very trees and their ancestors were once the source of the leaves used to produce Bay Rum cologne. I associate this warm scent of cloves with my mother's father. He and my grandmother vacationed at Caneel Bay Resort, established by the Rockefeller family but later destroyed by a hurricane in 2017, a place I'd not thought about for decades. Now, I breathed in the familiar, forgotten scent of my Scandinavian grandfather at family gatherings: Always more formal than his children and grandchildren, he would have been holding a cocktail, wearing an ascot, and smelling deliciously of Bay Rum cologne.

In the eighteenth and nineteenth centuries, this property was owned by Danes, and the land was worked by enslaved people. It is hard to imagine how grueling this life must have been, for the forest is now quiet and cool. The scent of cloves drifts in the air, and deer move through green leafy undergrowth like shadows. About a quarter mile up into the woods, at the end of a side path, lies the sarcophagus of the Danish wife, born in Saint Croix, of one of the early white landowners. She died at fifty-two in 1836, ten years before her husband would pass. While Anna lies in the woods with several smaller unmarked tombs around her, her husband is interred more grandly in a formal cemetery on Saint Thomas.

How did Anna Margarethe's family end up in Saint Croix? What kind of a life was it running a sugar factory in the hot, insect-infested forests of Saint John while her husband was often away? I couldn't help wondering, even in the unequal relationship between Anna and the workers on the farm, might there not also have been some complicated bonds of loyalty, friendship?

Standing in the forest, surrounded by trees with soft brown bark and slim trunks, I studied the stone box that reportedly holds Anna's remains. Not far away, the ocean hummed. And somehow, I summoned an idea of this woman and spoke to her: *I am here to remember you, to let you know in some strange way we are connected too. Our ancestors came from northern islands surrounded by the sea, but we ended up far from these places. Like me, you lived a life you may not have expected. I hope you are at peace in this lovely place in the woods.*

Finally, yesterday, we had a most glorious snorkeling adventure. A spotted eagle ray swam by me as if in flight; I dove down and looked eye-to-eye with two sea turtles. The water was exceptionally clear, and the sun was out. And what was most magical was swimming through enormous formations of tiny fish that moved in clouds, in wreath formations, some schools spinning apart then spiraling together like slow-moving tornadoes. The spiral formations seemed as esoteric as the double helix architecture of DNA winding and unwinding—and as intimate and friendly as the many, many small beings examining me with bright eyes and a silvery fish consciousness.

I am no more and no less. I am life—strange, shimmering, ever-changing. Beautiful.

I crave a sense of connection at this moment.

Connection to the twelve-year-old child I was and to the women who helped that girl through a difficult transition. *May I, too, be one of those women offering help or guidance to someone who lives after me.* I am connected to the pig-headed, emotionally explosive little boy, to a woman who lived in a jungle far from her native land, and even to a turtle, a ray, or one tiny member of a vast school of fish.

When I experience these moments of connection, I find peace and acceptance. A sense of enchantment and even *agalliasi*—joy— within this all too brief "wild and precious life."

Thank you again for the birthday wishes. What's going on with you in New York?

Chris

May 20, 2023
New York, New York

I ARRIVED HOME TODAY AS dusk closed in after a day as full and confusing and wonderful as any I can remember. It has me feeling alive, humming, conflicted, alert, and uncomfortable with how to integrate all these feelings.

I love how your experience of connection means a harmony of being in touch with the spirits of fish, recalcitrant children, expatriate wives, and anyone in need of guidance. The Wellesley motto, *non ministrari sed ministrare*, seems to be embodied in the thought that we fulfill our noblest usefulness (another college phrase) when we offer help or guidance to another. I agree that that is life, shimmering, strange, as changeable as the flash of silver in a school of fish, and as ineffably lovely.

The concept of integrity, of living in a way that is consciously true to one's belief system, has preoccupied me these past several weeks. After hearing a podcast, I ordered a book by Martha Beck called *The Way of Integrity*. I thought it was more philosophical and less self-help, but despite my irritation at being asked to engage in earnest exercises every chapter, it's been interesting. The premise is that all we need to know about how to live our lives in truth, which will also magically grant us better health and happiness, is contained within Dante's *Divine Comedy*.

So, I've been mulling over the concept of ordering one's behavior with the austere discipline of *only* doing and saying things that we know to be true. I've had a number of experiences this week that have led me to appreciate that level of intentionality and others where it's a little more complicated to sort out what I believe to be true.

I mentioned before that I had lunch about two weeks ago with a Turkish friend, a woman I had met about fifteen years ago through my ex-husband. They were both members of a group seeking a dialogue on Greek-Turkish reconciliation after the traumatic military incursions of the Greek army into Turkey after WWI and the subsequent defeat and horrifically violent slaughter and population exchange that ensued. She is an accomplished artisan in blown and molded glass, and I own several of her pieces; I knew that she had had a museum show of blown glass birds inspired by Louis de Bernières's novel *Birds without Wings*, but I wasn't aware of the depth of her empathy and imagination on the subject of exile, and her profound sensitivity to the experience of brutal, wrenching displacement.

We met as mothers, talked about our children, and about her collaboration with the Metropolitan Museum, which is carrying several of her pieces in their gift shop. She mentioned her latest work, a further extension inspired by the displacement of Syrians into Turkey, on the theme of the tiny, flightless, buffeted birds, victims of forces they cannot control and can barely respond to. She said she would send me the catalog from the current exhibition at the Sadberk Hanim Museum in Istanbul, entitled *After Utopia*. We parted after friendly banalities of how to get our kids in touch (her two daughters live in New York), and that was that.

But then I received the catalog, which is actually a work of art. It contains an imagined epilogue to Aristophanes' comedy *The Birds*, which expands on the original play's (satirical) premise of creating a utopia, Cloud Cuckoo Land, to escape the power of the gods. This, to me, is an amazing creative work in and of itself. The catalog is also a testament to the artwork, their place in history, their pathos, beauty, heartbreaking (in)significance, and the courage of the lonely voice exploring the pain of others with sensitivity. The narrative is in English, Karamanlidika Turkish (a language tradition preserved in Cappadocia, where Ottoman Christians spoke Turkish but wrote it in Greek characters) and ancient Greek. It acknowledges one of the odder chapters of this great civilizational upheaval that is today visible in the courtyard of the Baloukli Monastery, on the outskirts of Istanbul, which is paved with the tombstones brought from Cappadocia to what was still Constantinople in the 1920s; the gravestones are inscribed in Greek characters, but the language is Turkish.

What makes it more evocative is that Baloukli Monastery is intimately associated with a poignant legend about the fall of Constantinople, the Queen City of the thousand-year empire, in May of 1453. The monastery is located far outside the walled city, and the monks believed that the Theodosian walls, which had endured for nearly a thousand years, would still protect the embattled, shrunken, besieged Byzantine empire. A rider came to the monastery, breathless, shattered, his horse lathered, shouting, "They've taken the city!" The monk scoffed, leaning over his frying pan, "Impossible! It's more likely that the fish I am frying will take life and swim again!" The legend, of course, is that the fish leapt from the pan back into the Bosphorus, sealing the fate of the city. To this day, the holy water spring at Baloukli contains carp swimming around.

All of which is a very roundabout way of saying that I was touched beyond words at my friend's exercise in imagining the connection between the pain of the displaced Syrians and that of the Ottoman Christians who found themselves torn from their homes of a thousand years back in 1922, fully one hundred years ago. And as much as I hesitate to ascribe a unique capacity for empathy to those of us who have been privileged to be mothers, I feel that it endows us with a particular ability to feel a particular pain.

This led into Mother's Day, a holiday that I used to enjoy when I was a kid celebrating my own mother but have always found performative as a mother. It's now one I find particularly difficult since it bangs up against feelings and internal challenges (Was I a good mother? Good enough? Not good enough to keep my child alive?) as well as a resentment of the commercial interests expert at manipulating guilt to make us buy shit. I was working at the Castle that day and managed to ignore most of it, only wincing when one of the doormen at my building enthusiastically wished me a happy Mother's Day. He's met Yannis; he meant well, and I smiled as I winced.

This emotionally fraught week then led into my choral concert, an unmitigated joy and an experience of deep gratitude. The music (Faure's *Requiem* and Mozart's *Coronation Mass*) alone was transporting, and in addition, I had my own cheering section from family, high school, college, and early work colleagues. It didn't feel inconsistent or dishonest to sing the liturgy of a Catholic Mass, including a creed I no longer believe in, perhaps because the most profound prayer is the universal plea, *dona nobis pacem*—grant us peace.

We went for beer and potato pancakes afterwards at the Heidelberg, a stalwart German bar on 2nd Avenue and 86th Street, where my parents used to go in the mid-1950s after Fordham University Glee Club concerts. It felt like an ineffable connection, a cosmic circle being closed.

The week was capped by two profound art experiences—the first at the Met, visiting the new exhibition on van Gogh's cypresses with a new friend, another mother who has lost a child to suicide. The intensity and beauty of the artworks were magnified, for both of us, by the intensity of the beauty and the pain on display.

The truism is that if you've known one person who's died by suicide, you've known one person; there is no universal characteristic that unites or explains the why. The lives and struggles of our children are heartbreakingly varied. The only thing that all parents who have lost children to suicide seem to have in common is the perception that our children felt everything more intensely than other people. Greg was transported by music. He danced unselfconsciously and with extraordinary feeling; he was incapable of regulating his emotional response to beauty and, apparently, to pain. So, seeing van Gogh's utter nakedness, painting on leave from the asylum where he was confined for his own safety, this heartbreakingly vulnerable capacity for expression resonated for both of us in a way that felt both profound and futile.

The second was today, visiting one art installation and one art show near the Brooklyn Navy Yard with my son and his girlfriend, who is a madly talented designer. The art installation was one of her projects at the Pratt Institute, where she's earning her master's degree in communication design, which I find both cool and intimidating, and the art show, called *The Other Art Fair*, was just a wonderful romp into about one hundred different artists' tiny booths of works for sale. I felt both flattered and slightly flustered to be invited, but Maria Alexia is lovely and her aesthetic is beautiful, original and authentic, and she's entertained (or at least not alarmed) by the lunacy that passes for my thought process. Yannis has known her since high school, so we all speak Greek and English with the same fluency, and I love the chaotic concatenation of language that is Greeklish, where we can shift between languages three times in the same sentence, make one-word cultural references that have us all snickering, and find the exact word, that exists in only one of the languages, for the zeitgeist feeling of the moment. It just felt whole, in some weird way, but whole in the *kintsugi* sense, where the fracture lines of the repaired structure were visible.

We traveled together to Brooklyn from the Upper East Side by subway, but Yannis and Maria Alexia were staying in Brooklyn, babysitting a friend's recalcitrant cats. I elected to return via the East

River ferry from the Navy Yard to East 90th Street, a forty-minute journey that zig-zags across the river from DUMBO to 34th Street, Long Island City to Roosevelt Island, Astoria, and finally, the end of Carl Schurz Park, just south of Asphalt Green and north of Gracie Mansion. It was drizzling and gray when I started, but the rain soon stopped, so I braved the upper deck, resigned to sitting on a slightly puddled seat but enjoying the dusk, colored in the grays and yellows of El Greco's *View of Toledo* and the fresh scent of the river. The ferry captain's skill was evident in the apparent absence of effort; he had to spin the boat around 180 degrees to dock on Roosevelt Island, and he did it with the elegance of a hockey stop, skidding ever so elegantly in a half-circle, gliding smoothly against the current to face south, then reverse out again.

As we approached the final station, I felt overwhelmed by conflicting emotions. I felt joy and wholeness in where I am now in my life, a sense that I am living in absolute integrity with what I want to embrace. But I could not embrace this joy without sadness and guilt, the sensation that this full, rich life, brimming with art, ideas, music, and connection, only exists because my son took his own life.

Greg's final email was entitled "Sacrifice." His death was, in his perception, a liberation for himself and a gift to his family, releasing himself from a painful terminal illness and us from what he perceived to be the burden of caring about him. I am cognizant of the love in him that made him determined to bestow this gift. But I am haunted by the sense that I should have known and should have been able to make him understand that this was not the solution. I would give up all of what I have built to return to the day before, to show him that nothing would be worth losing him, to convince him that I would gladly put up with whatever burden there might be if it only meant that he would be whole and happy. But I can't change what has happened. When I feel overwhelmed and can't get past the knot in my throat, I listen to the music of the piper who played the threnody at Greg's funeral. The pipes and drums together, the clanging that is torment and triumph, make me smile and cry at the same time.

Love,
J

May 30, 2023
Breckenridge, Colorado

WE WERE IN MOAB FOR two days, biking in that towered and otherworldly landscape. Then, we spent another two days with a winemaker friend and his science-writer wife in Cedaredge, Colorado, also known among wine nerds as the highest elevation in the northern hemisphere where *Vitis vinifera*—the "noble" or classic French grapes—will grow (6,800 feet).

Once, after our formal working lives had come to an end, Alan and I were two people who spent a great deal of time lazily reading, debating over who was right about some pointless subject, or napping on the couch. But we have been on the move much of the time since last winter. The sad loss of Luke in early December and the ever-present uncertainty of my health have made us edgy and restless. It is too easy in familiar surroundings to remember how it was when there were three of us. And when I was healthy.

But we are home now, back from our road trip to Utah and western Colorado. With the return of spring and the appearance of greenery and new life on the mountain, my mood has shifted. And all of a sudden, these months of movement from place to place to place have got me longing for stillness. Time to sift through all the past months' experiences and piece things together. Time to integrate.

I continue to think a lot about connection. Have I already mentioned that the largest and heaviest living creature on earth is an aspen grove in Utah named Pando? We may see this grove as individual trees, but in fact, the living being here is the grove itself, an estimated 80,000 years old, that multiplies and expands beneath the earth.

> Pando is believed to be the largest, most dense organism ever found at nearly 13 million pounds. The clone spreads over 106 acres, consisting of over 40,000 individual trees.
> —United States Department of Agriculture

Each individual tree, I imagine, reaches back into the past for wisdom and sustenance, and each makes offerings toward the future. It implies that a life force continues—to me, that a little part of each of us persists—even as some trees die and provide nutrients to others that sprout up through the soil as young saplings.

The aspen grove is a wonderful metaphor for connection and integration. Here, just up the hill from our house, we also have a huge grove of aspens that continues to expand every year. I like to walk up the logging road and stand among the slim, white tree trunks. All the trees are related, from oldest to youngest, sharing nutrients, messages about their environment, and perhaps even a tree version of care and affection for one another.

Back in mid-May, on our way home from Saint John, we stopped in Miami to see my niece Amanda and her husband. We then took a short jaunt up to West Palm Beach with plans to stay with my brother and his family.

I'm extremely close to Amanda. She and I share a curiosity about ideas, a love of books and nice restaurants, and professional ambition. I witness in Amanda the same intense desire to see as much of the world as possible that I have felt throughout my life—but particularly as a young woman.

On this visit, Amanda pulled out a collection of photo albums that her father—my sister's first husband—had recently passed on to her. They were photos of Amanda from infancy through her parents' divorce when she was about nine or ten: "Auntie Chris, do you want to see the photos Dad sent me?"

What caught me off guard and moved me to tears was that I was also in many, many of these photos with Amanda. I was that much a part of her life from the beginning. As time had gone by, I'd forgotten this.

A few days later, I was also surprised when my sixteen-year-old nephew, my brother's son, cautiously perched on the arm of the couch I was curled upon in their living room. Nick began hesitantly to talk to me about his college plans, warming with enthusiasm until he actually slid down off the couch arm and landed right next to me: "I'm thinking of going to law school, or maybe business school. But I'm still not sure if I want to be a coach or maybe a real estate agent." The plans were a little unformed, but his enthusiasm for a future full of possibility was real.

These days, parents don't always see college as cost-effective or necessary—college has become so expensive, and politics have worked to create uncertainty among parents about the value of higher education. My experience at Wellesley was and remains one of immeasurable value to me, so I have encouraged college for all the kids in my family. The experience of my nephew wanting to communicate his excitement about his possible future(s) to me made me so happy. Perhaps I had touched the future and had an impact.

Both of these encounters forced me to think hard about the wall of noncommunication between my sister and myself. My family has a long history of various members taking offense or behaving with vicious cruelty toward one another, cutting each other off and then playing the role of victim. My sister lives ten minutes from my brother; she and I have not spoken since 2021. Political differences and the COVID epidemic only made the likelihood of communication more remote.

Despite my concern about the possibility of another angry inter-action with my sister, I contacted her about having lunch with my brother's wife and me. I decided that I do not want to be a sick or thwarted aspen tree that passes on to the youngsters in my family cruelty, victimhood, or a refusal to communicate. I would like to take a step toward breaking that cycle and transmitting something better, healthier.

We three women had our brief lunch, which was coolly cordial. In small increments, my relationship with my sister has improved since that meeting. And while I meant to do something that might be a positive example to the kids, in the end, I also allowed myself to let go of a certain amount of anxiety and stress around family rela-tionships. I opened a door and gave myself a measure of freedom.

How have the experiences of these past months shaped me? And what can *I* make of *them*? One definition of integrity is "the state of being whole, undivided." I like the idea of the aspen grove as an ancient and whole being, linking not only the past with the future but bringing together—making use of—everything in its environment. My Dear Friend, this creative conversation of ours has given wings to that grounded bird—stripped of its ability to fly—that I felt I was a year ago. Allowed me to make connections, communicate experiences of beauty and joy, and create meaning from anger, despair, fear, and loss.

 And it continues to be a path to wholeness.
 With love,
 Chris

Summer

June 9, 2023
New York, New York

I HAVE BEEN MUSING OVER the organism that is family and connection, and I agree that it's wonderfully affirming to feel like a contributing cell that sustains while it is sustained. That was one of the emotions I returned with from our fortieth Wellesley reunion, where I reconnected with dear friends, crossed orbits with women I like and don't really know, and walked in the early morning stillness of that spectacular campus.

One of our classmates, Mary, set up weekly Zoom calls during the pandemic with about ten or fifteen classmates. I wasn't equally close to all of them in college, but there was a core of those who have been "ride or die" friends for all these years, as well as those who I was happy to see. Mary was the weekly host for over two years, and the rest of us hopped in and out as time and motivation dictated. The pandemic, for me, of course, was a period of extraordinary upheaval, and this was a noncompulsory lifeline that kept me tethered to sanity. It was so wonderful to see these people in person, to give strong hugs, to thank them for being so important in my life, and to feel that I was important to them, too.

There was a Saturday night dance party after our class dinner, and I suspect the DJ, a very cool-looking, dread-locked guy, anticipated a sedate evening with the gray-haired crowd he saw around the tables. But he started the set with "Proud Mary," and nobody sat down for two and a half hours. He was grinning ear to ear as we begged for one more song and gyrated with more enthusiasm than talent to "Rock Lobster."

There is a unique joy among women dancing with women—groups form, break, reform, split once again, and it all feels like some mad cell division from a science documentary, but with moments of absolute alignment and belonging. I have always loved to dance, but when I last danced at my friend's daughter's wedding last summer, it felt perfunctory, a sort of forced gaiety. This felt wonderful.

Sunday morning, after a night in the "new" dorms that reminded me why communal bathrooms are something you tolerate at a much younger age, I went for a walk down by the chapel, down to the lake and Tupelo Point. I startled two rabbits, watched darting jays and sparrows, and saw a mother swan with three cygnets paddling serenely in the cove by the Hunnewell gardens. It was a Mary Oliver moment of grace in nature and put me in the right mood to attend the service of remembrance at the chapel, gazing once more at the luminous Tiffany windows. Mercedes's name was among those of our classmates who have died since our last reunion, and I thought of how vibrant, how optimistic and resilient she was. I miss her. Then, as I probably should have anticipated, I was incapable of more than silent tears as I thought of my boy. I tried to take part in the responsive call to remembrance, written by Sylvan Kamens and Rabbi Jack Riemer, a simple, reverential antiphon, but no sound would come out. I'm wiping away tears as I write this. But I was sitting next to Sarah, whom I met on the first day of freshman year on the same corridor of the second floor of Shafer, and the presence of my irrepressible, honest, and loving friend was consolation.

Your information about Pando got me to contemplate my place in the multigenerational web of my own family, very different from yours, I think. I had a chance this week to spend four days in Amagansett with my mother, who has never been anything but a rock of support, love, determination, and joy. I realize how saccharine that sounds, but it's true. She is also responsible for the genetic configuration of my brain, which leaps from topic to topic, making vague connections between apparently disparate ideas and events. Mom's brain is also run by a pack of unruly otters who haven't taken their Ritalin, and our conversations bounce in happy chaotic disarray like the steel ball in a pinball machine. Her command of information, from history to current political events to literature, is formidable—I love talking to her. But it's the first year, truly, where my eighty-six-year-old mother seems, well, old. She's a little less steady on her feet (stairs are harder), and she frequently misplaces her keys and glasses. Her gardening stamina is still impressive, nonetheless, and after two days of combat pruning that left us both covered in bruises and random scratches and cuts from diving into juniper bushes and eradicating the clinging vines threatening to strangle the forsythia, we were both sore and very tired. We agreed to take the third day off, but on our way to a sedate lunch in Southampton, we "had" to stop in at the furniture thrift shop run by ARF, the Animal Rescue Fund.

I knew she had an ulterior motive, which was to find a table to replace a humble little pine gate-leg table I had acquired last year. I was very proud of having stripped and refinished it, and I use it as my primary dining, sitting, and mail-dumping table. Mom did not like this table, in keeping with her long history of irrational but firm prejudices on inconsequential matters. And as it happens, there was a particularly gorgeous American Empire table with a folding top and lustrous, if neglected, mahogany veneer.

Mom whispered, "It's been here since March; they'll take less than the tagged price." She was right. I made a ridiculously low offer which was immediately accepted. When I explained that I would have to pick it up the next day since the car was stuffed to the gills with juniper clippings and the dump was closed, the owner offered to let us dump the clippings in his empty dumpster just to get the damn table out of his shop. I was fleetingly suspicious that the table was possessed by demons, but it's beautiful and, thus far, has not required an exorcism.

My mother was ecstatic and I was delighted. Once we got back to her place, we attacked it with Old English furniture polish and a scratch-eradicator called the Tibet Almond Stick. She rummaged on my father's workbench, found a bag of tiny veneer patches and veneer glue and a couple of spare scalpel blades (don't ask; my dad was a pack rat), and told me how to prepare the template of the patch. I will attempt the project of the tiny patch job sometime in the coming weeks; the fact that we can do this together, to some degree, makes it all the more special. A year ago, Mom came into the city and replaced the fabric on four dining chairs we had purchased at ARF. I don't know how many more years of projects we have ahead, but what strength, and beauty, and sustaining joy she brings to our aspen patch.

The next generation of our Pando brings me equivalent joy, as well as profound gratitude and relief. Yannis went to Greece last week, spoke to his father for the first time in nearly two years, attended his cowardly cousin's wedding, and navigated multiple cross-currents of family drama. He came back emotionally wrung out but stronger, grounded, and more certain of his own inner illumination. His anger has been spent, but his boundaries are firmly in place. To explain the characterization of the cousin, Yannis had been unceremoniously demoted from best man to simple guest with no explanation other than the suspicion that his cousin was afraid of offending his influential uncle. I was not invited to the wedding at all; I would not have attended, and they could have saved face but chose to burn bridges.

And to conclude this entry, which is fast becoming an epic, I want to share a quotation from René Magritte, brought to my attention by the inimitable, gifted, splendid humanist Maria Popova. It's about choosing joy.

Our mental universe (which contains all we know, feel or are afraid of in the real world we live in) may be enchanting, happy, tragic, comic, etc. We are capable of transforming it and giving it a charm, which makes life more valuable. More valuable since life becomes more joyful, thanks to the extraordinary effort needed to create this charm. . . . We must go in search of enchantment.

Here's to enchantment,
Love,
J

June 20, 2023
Breckenridge, Colorado

I AM STILL THINKING ABOUT Pando: connections near and far, recent or long ago. And this is a roundabout way of getting to the story of a decorative platter, a snapshot of which was sent to me recently by Kathie Aldrich, the owner of Polly's Pancake Parlor in Sugar Hill, New Hampshire.

In 1979, despite my mother's firm objection to restaurant work for her daughters, I spent my last New Hampshire summer before college as a hostess in Polly's Pancake Parlor.

"If I repent of anything, it is very likely to be my good behavior. What demon possessed me that I behaved so well?" I'd been enthralled by these lines from *Walden* in my senior year of high school. I was restless and couldn't wait to leave home and go to college! Making my own money seemed like a first step toward freedom and away from my childhood with its emphasis on good behavior. Admittedly, it would be difficult to imagine a gentler act of rebellion than my insistence on a summer job in a local pancake parlor. Even so, my determination was initially received by my parents with consternation and alarm.

But the Aldrich family were old-time Sugar Hill people, I argued; how could my parents really object? Finally, Kathie's mother, Nancy Aldrich, took pity on me and hired me. For all I know, she may have actually spoken to my mother to reassure her. And I am pretty sure it was Kathie, about my age but far more mature, who got stuck being my "supervisor."

As driven as I was in 1979 to plunge headlong into my future, forty years later, I became equally obsessed with returning in my imagination to that era of the 1970s. The past, with its lazy summers spent in New Hampshire seemed magical to me, now that I was in my mid-fifties. For years, I wrote rough sketches about my childhood in our rambling summer home beneath tall cedar trees at the foot of the White Mountains. Finally, in late 2017, I began the story of a young woman from New York whose path collides with a local young man from New Hampshire as she struggles to create a future very different from what her family envisioned.

Sometimes, people diagnosed with an illness that will cut short their life become fiercely determined to achieve personal goals: They set their sights on completing a triathlon, immerse themselves in poetry, climb Mount Everest, learn to spend hours in prayer or meditation. *Yes, Death, you will win in the end. But while I am here, I will do what I believe I came here to do; I will inhabit this life to the fullest.* For me, during those grim and exhausting days of radiation and chemo in May and June of 2022, completing this story and seeing it published became my Mount Everest.

In August of 2022, Alan and I stopped at Polly's on our way to Maine and gave Kathie Aldrich a copy of the published book, which features a scene in her family's restaurant. Kathie kindly offered to order the book for Polly's gift shop. Then, hesitating, she gave me the terrible news: The house my family had owned, which had inspired the grand estate Cedaredge in my novel, had been torn down by new owners who presumably wanted something slick and modern.

Stunned, Alan and I drove up the Birches Road to the now-barren property. We got out of the car, and Alan put his arms around me and whispered, "I'm so sorry." And while I felt shock and anger, the strongest feeling I experienced was—to my complete surprise—one of, well, enlightenment.

I could finally understand that the house I had loved, with all our family and its drama, was a house in my memory. Being confronted with the pile of dirt where this beautiful stone and shingle summer cottage once meandered beneath the now-felled cedar trees was a brutal wake up call to the ephemeral nature of material reality. Because of my illness, because of my sometimes-pathological hand-wringing over the past, this was a message I needed to accept. And now, somehow, I did.

This week, almost a year later, Kathie has been in touch and sent me an email with a photo attached: a snapshot of a decorative plate which she found among her deceased mother's, Nancy's, treasured belongings. The image on this plate is of this very house that my family owned on Sugar Hill. And, as it turns out, Kathie discovered that the house was also owned at one time by the Aldrich family. It even had a name: The Wayside. And while this house is now gone, in its place, I sense my deeper connection to Kathie, to her mother Nancy, who gave me a job and a taste of financial independence, and to the memory of a unique and beautiful time and place in the White Mountains of New Hampshire. The house lives now where it belongs: in my memory and in my imagination.

Last weekend, Saturday, June 10, Alan and I attended the Colorado Book Award ceremony. My publisher and her husband accompanied us, along with a friend I love to walk and discuss writing with, and her partner. The novel I had struggled to complete was chosen as a winner of the 2023 Colorado Book Award. The award feels like one of the biggest accomplishments of my life. Like seeing my flag planted on Mount Everest.

Perhaps even more important, this moment of recognition has offered me the grace of discovering the capacity within myself to cherish a connection to my past (symbolized by a treasured platter with a painting of a beautiful family house) while embracing the present, where I belong now at this time in my life: my home with Alan in the Rocky Mountains of Colorado.

Love,
Chris

June 23, 2023
New York, New York

I WAS SO SORRY FOR you to hear that your summer house, the touchstone of so many memories and formative experiences, had been torn down. I'm impressed that you were able to perceive its loss immediately as a release from the obligation of homage, in a way—that the structure's absence could sort of distill its meaning into the experiences rather than the physical walls. And how lovely that its talisman exists in the form of a platter! I wonder if you would be able to find other plates with the image of Wayside House.

Upon reflection, I think I had such a visceral reaction to the shock of the loss because of the changes my ex has wrought in our beach house in Agiannaki, where you and Alan spent part of your honeymoon. This house was a work of love and a lot of legwork on my part. I had collaborated closely with the architect to build a house that would nestle into the environment, be welcoming to wet swimsuits and lazy breakfasts, have spaces that would encourage sociability but also offer privacy, satisfy my husband's ambitions to host multiple guests, but not overwhelm the peaceful landscape it would occupy. Furnishings were chosen for comfort and durability (here, the Athens Ikea played a major role) or for quirkiness and uniqueness, including a wall of antique tools on the stone-faced living room wall.

From 2005 through the summer of 2020, and especially after our separation in 2016, this house was my refuge, my sanctuary, my touchstone. After I left Greece in a fog of grief and anger in late 2020,

I determined that I could not bear the idea of sharing it with my ex. The divorce agreement reached a Solomonic decision—neither of us would get to keep it; it would be sold, and the proceeds split. Real estate tangles and land registry laws in Greece being what they are, no immediate offers at the (high) price that I set were forthcoming, so the house is still there and still in his name. I spent a week there in June 2022 and found it almost unbearable. The "improvements" made by another woman's hand in new linens, a new bed in what had been our bedroom, and other decor changes that erased my sons' presence from their shared bedroom bore the unmistakable hand of that woman friend whose green crystal glasses I had smashed. I was told recently that their relationship is now public, and I feel a certain relief that "Camilla" is now official, sort of how you felt when you found that your home had been bulldozed. Odd, but more liberating than hurtful. My anger has also mellowed, and I have proposed that rather than sell the property, part of the title should be transferred to Yannis, who can decide what he wants to do with it after his father dies.

Other healing threads seem to be coming together within my family as well. Maria Alexia, whose many artistic talents include woodworking skills, agreed to "help" me with the veneer replacement project by doing the whole thing. She's encouraged Yannis to explore his desire to make things and has given him lessons in artistic welding and turning wood on a lathe. My father taught woodworking skills to my brothers and built a boat model with Yannis in the summer of 2010, but my ex did not come from a family with any interest in working with their hands; I was the one with the toolbox who requested a drill for a wedding gift. My mother has saved an enormous trunk of a beautiful cherry tree they had to cut down about twenty years ago, as my younger brother wanted the wood, but he's never figured out an easy way to get this tree trunk out to San Francisco, where he lives. So, Mom, hearing that Yannis might take lessons in turning bowls on a lathe, was delighted to offer him slices of the cherry wood—material that ties him to his grandfather, has intrinsic beauty, and fulfills his hunger to make things.

A quick postscript: I wrote most of this two days ago, a bit surprised that what I thought I wanted to say wasn't what came out. Yesterday morning, I woke up with a black "floater" in my left eye, which rapidly morphed into a viscous, dirty curtain across my vision. Googling the symptoms sent me into a (justifiable) panic, and by six in the morning, I was at the Lenox Hill emergency room. After being assessed for craziness (which I fully understand is necessary at an NYC hospital early in the morning), they sent me down to Manhattan Eye and Ear, and three physicians later, I was in the very reassuring, kind hands of a "vitreo-retinal fellow" who lasered the torn retina back in place. Yikes.

I took the bus home—I needed time in the anonymity of public transportation to process the amazing speed at which I lost my assumptions of rude, imperturbable health and shifted to utter panic, worry mixed with irritation at the inevitable hospital bingo of being asked the same questions twenty times, and ultimately gratitude for the fact that, six hours after I woke up with a potentially blinding complication, I was on my way home all fixed. Amazing. I realized how lucky I am to live where I do and to have the people around me who sped to offer support, transport, names of ophthalmologists, and general concern. I was especially touched to answer a call in the early evening from an unknown number and find, on the other end, the PA who had seen me that morning at Lenox Hill and counseled me to go to the specialists—she was worried about me! And they say New Yorkers aren't kind.

Resilience in the face of loss and change, and the ability to recognize when it's time to give things up,

Love,

J

July 1, 2023
Breckenridge, Colorado

OH, JANE, HOW SCARY! LIFE shocks us like a bolt of electricity that flips the switch from a bright assumption of good health to a sudden, dark confrontation with a serious medical condition. I don't think there is a convincing way to describe this so that another person can really understand the disbelief, disorientation, the way it messes with your emotions. If life's capacity to pull the rug out from under us were a story, it would go like this: The heroine we have come to love and identify with walks blithely through the forest on her way home after a day's adventures. Suddenly, she falls into a hole never to be seen again. The End. The reader would be outraged, betrayed—impossible! Who wrote this story?—and throw the book across the room.

I am so relieved that you received quick and compassionate care, and that you are on the mend.

A few weeks ago, I planted petunias in the window boxes beside the stairs that lead up to our porch. As a girl in New Hampshire and then throughout the stretches of my adult life when I lived in a northern climate, I've performed this ritual of petunia planting to signify the beginning of summer. Except for last year. Last year, Alan and I spent May and June in Denver; generous friends lent us their house while I submitted to daily radiation treatments at the university hospital in the morning; in the afternoons, I struggled through pages of proofreading. When we came back to Breckenridge on the weekends, I was too exhausted to do anything but sleep.

During that time in Denver, Alan tried to keep my spirits up by planning a few manageable excursions: to the zoo, the botanical gardens, to Michael's craft shop to buy some silk flowers for the flower boxes at home. With cloth blooms, the boxes wouldn't look so empty or forlorn, he consoled me. I did not want to hurt or discourage Alan by telling him that every time I walked down those steps and passed the flower boxes with their lifeless orange pom-poms, I was reminded of how sick I was, of what I had lost.

But this year, I planted petunias again. Now I get up early, go outside, sit on the porch with my coffee, and watch the red and purple and magenta blossoms fill up with morning sunlight. I water them, pluck the dead blossoms so that new buds will form, and step out of the way as the hummingbird comes buzzing in for nectar. I feel well again. I can't say what is happening inside me, but the way I feel . . . I feel good.

I look like my old self (including, unfortunately, the ten pounds I have put back on, after losing them during radiation and chemo). Earlier this week, I was on my mountain bike; yesterday, I took a long hike. If you didn't know, you'd assume I was a healthy person. And that has come with its own host of issues for me. Because nothing has changed about the prognosis for this disease. And except for moments by the ocean in Saint John, not a day goes by that I am unaware of this fact, even in my dreams. I am terribly sad at times and often easy to anger.

If I don't pay attention to my emotions, I'll still find myself going from zero to one hundred, fast, with anger and frustration. I am angry that it is harder to read (I listen to a lot of audiobooks now); I am angry about being interrupted and immediately forgetting what I had been doing right before the interruption. I am angry that my awareness of my illness has made me less independent and more fearful of driving and being out in the world.

I am angry at the developers across the road from us, cutting down all the trees—the wanton killing of trees, birds, animals, and their habitat is intolerable! Don't they understand how terribly wrong it is to create more death, destruction? More suffering? When I rail against this new development to our neighbors, I see in their faces that I am too strident, too filled with fury.

I can't expect people to remember or to be thinking about my health condition all the time (or at all), the way I do.

My emotions are even more knotted where my family is involved. My aunt and I got together for the first time in nearly four years last week. When she reached out to me with a card—"let's try to put the past behind us," she wrote—I agreed to go for a hike. Arriving at our house, she came up very close to me, peered at my face, and said, "You look the same." Almost as if I had been fooling everyone for the past year, or so it seemed to me.

Did her turns of phrase hold a note of suspicion? As if I had been trying to hide things from her, but she was too clever and had found me out? "I *know* you wrote a book because my friend in Vail got a copy from one of your friends," she informed me. "I *know* you sold your house in Palisade because someone I know bought it from you." And "I *heard* you were in Saint John—for *how many* weeks?"

I was wary and, later, unreasonably angry: Had she expected me to look sicker? Should I have made sure she knew all the ins-and-outs of my life? Our adult relationship has had an undercurrent of blame and guilt running through it. She speaks of her many disappointments, the hard knocks, while my life seems so much better. Should I feel guilty that, despite a terminal illness, I went breezing off to Saint John? During this first face-to-face meeting of ours since my mother's death, resentment got the better of me.

The bright, happy thought of petunias has pulled me up out of bed early this morning, and I settle on the porch with my coffee. Our acre of mostly trees and undergrowth is home to so many animals and birds. A chickadee lands on my hand, fluttering her wings in that "Feed me!" behavior that is so ridiculously cute I want to laugh or cry with tenderness as I offer her some seeds. There is the wren singing on top of the house that he finally convinced his mate to accept, swallows, blue birds on the other side of the house, fox, moose, rabbits, and several silly chipmunks. When I activate my Merlin Bird ID app, it detects over a dozen different types of birds singing. The morning is heavenly.

I started by writing how hard it is to imagine being sick when you are healthy. But I am also finding it hard to put down the useless burden of anger and struggle and to imagine the calm simplicity—the lightness—of nonstriving happiness. Unlike illness, which has come at me, like it or not, my state of mind is something I choose. I can't take on the responsibility of pleasing everyone else, but I can make small positive changes in my own life and outlook. None of us can do that for another; it is a big enough job trying to do it for ourselves.

Now, a hummingbird rockets up to me, pauses, checks me out, then darts to the big red petunias in the flower boxes. I flip the switch. Today, right now, these vibrant flowers of summer are what is real. And so, in this moment, is my happiness.

Thinking of you and hoping for the continued improvement of your vision and no more scary trips to the emergency room!

XX
Chris

July 2, 2023
New York, New York

THE CHOICE IS STARK: Do I suffer, or do I refuse to suffer? In the taxi on the way to the Eye & Ear Infirmary last Saturday, I kept thinking of the words of Viktor Frankl about stimulus and response. I didn't remember them exactly, as I was trying to control my rising panic, but I've looked them up:

> Between the stimulus and response, there is a space. And in that space lies our freedom and power to choose our responses. In our response lies our growth and our freedom.

This quote has popped into my head in various situations over the years, from difficult spots in my marriage to Greg's funeral, at moments when I felt least in control.

The challenge, as you so eloquently put it, is to put down the anger and struggle, the sense of cosmically unfair helplessness, and choose to imagine, and maybe to embody, nonstriving happiness. To choose my state of mind. To plant petunias.

At moments when I am happiest in my new life, there are often unbidden images of guilt. I woke up early this morning from a recurring dream of having lost Greg in some crowded place. Last night, he was an adolescent, probably late-teens, in a crowded downtown Athens. I woke up worried, then relieved, then bereft. I remembered how much he loved being in Amagansett for the Fourth of July—the fireworks, hot dogs, beach bonfire in a bucket, s'mores, corn on the cob, sandy brownies—the works.

I know it makes absolutely no sense to feel guilty for living, for accepting his sacrifice. I didn't have a say in the matter, and to live my life in an endless gyre of self-flagellation would desecrate his memory. But, sometimes, choosing happiness is fucking hard.

So, I will mentally transfer myself, and you, I hope, to one of my happy places: the temple of all things New York, the Rainbow Ace Hardware store on 1st Avenue and 76th Street. I discovered Ace in 2017 when I needed some things to help Yannis move into his second apartment. This was a fifth-floor one-bedroom walkup but an improvement from his first apartment, a tiny studio over a loud doggy daycare center. The move was eventful because between choosing the new place and signing the lease, he was hospitalized with complications of septic appendicitis, and I flew on an hour's notice from Athens to his hospital bedside, where he stayed for a week on intravenous antibiotics. Between hospital visits, I packed up the studio apartment, dismantled furniture, cleaned obsessively enough to ensure that he got his deposit back, and then helped reassemble everything in the new space.

You first go to Ace for mundane things like packing tape and boxes; little do you know that you are entering Aladdin's cave. It is deceptively huge, encompassing most of the block of 1st Avenue between 76th and 75th Streets. Between the main floor and the basement, the sheer variety and usefulness of its stock is nothing short of astonishing. Nails, hooks, bathtub plugs, plumbing fixtures, fishing wire, any tool you might ever need short of a band saw. Storage boxes, hangers, pillows, bathroom supplies, roach and mouse extermination supplies; blackout curtains, stepladders, trash cans, ceramic pots, potting soil, obscure brands of furniture polish and cleaning supplies; excellent pots and pans, Italian espresso makers, sushi mats, butter dishes and mandolin slicers (how did I make it to nearly sixty-two years of age without discovering the joy of the mandolin slicer?!?). Ace also carries my favorite shampoo, great coffee, licorice, French-milled lavender and mint soap, and silly socks with watermelon-eating otters on them. It is staffed by people with a mystical knowledge of the thousands of products they sell, capable of sending you to the right aisle and the right shelf the first time. If Ace Hardware doesn't sell it, I don't think you need it.

I visit this store the way normal women go to Bloomingdales—I go in for one thing I ostensibly need, spend up to an hour happily perusing the various sections, and come out with at least five things I cannot live without. I went this week to find a plastic wash basin for soaking woolen sweaters, and came out with a collapsible basin (everything is calibrated around the Jenga space requirements of the average New York apartment), a stain remover that worked a treat on a stubborn mark that had lurked on a pashmina for some time, a small cooler bag for trips to the beach, and organic fruit-flavored gummy bears. And the checkout ladies smile and call you "honey."

So, after work today, where I will spend my Sunday happily directing New Yorkers and tourists through Belvedere Castle, I will head out to Amagansett to spend the Fourth of July with my mom, my son, and his girlfriend, carrying my new cooler bag and missing my boy. I will try to choose gratitude, joy and happiness, sponsored in part by Ace Hardware.

Happy Fourth,
XO
J

July 9, 2023
Breckenridge, Colorado

HARDWARE STORES ARE A PLACE where, no matter the problem or crisis, a solution of some sort can be found. My mother loved hardware stores, too. Remember Scarsdale Hardware in the Harwood Building? Mom enjoyed making things and fixing things. I suspect—no, I am certain—that she also liked the gruff, manly staff with their "can-do" attitude at the hardware store. When I read your piece, I couldn't help but visualize your Manhattan Ace Hardware as a place of comfort and reassurance.

We talked this week when I was having yet another meltdown over the question of "shoulds" in my life. When I reread many of my letters to you, I see how, at sixty-two and with a diagnosis of a brain tumor, I *still* feel incredibly tangled up in confusion over "shoulds." While last spring there was little question of how to spend my time when it came to completing a project I had spent five years working on, now I am faced with . . . living. Just living. How do I make this one "wild and precious life" count?

Throughout our lives, plenty of people are standing by—parents, friends, bosses, marketing experts, doctors, Facebook or Instagram connections—to suggest or downright tell us (in words and pictures) what we should be doing, thinking, feeling, eating, how we should look, and more. Ironically, if we are not being bombarded with these messages, if we have a few moments of peace and quiet . . . well, then we search these messages out! (*What the fuck* should *I be doing? I have no clue. Let me check Instagram.*)

And this continues, even if you have a terminal illness. Only now, the messages are both more urgent and more confusingly contradictory. And how are you ever going to know what will turn out to be right for you? After all, this is not a scenario where you can get much feedback.

Should I . . . .

- Travel the world and fulfill a "bucket list" *or* retreat like a monk and seek quiet and meditation?
- Release attachment to the future *or* ruminate over "my legacy"?
- Let go because I am in acceptance *or* hold on because I am a fighter?
- Clarify with the hospital chaplain/death doula thoughts about my pending "transition" and death *or* focus on living "my best life now"?
- Cut out sugar (and meat, dairy, gluten, alcohol . . .)?
- Mend difficult relationships *or* avoid toxic people?
- Ignore what others tell me *or* accept that everyone will tell me to ignore what everyone tells me: "It's up to you!" (Wait, do I ignore that?)

I cannot erase from my memory the confusion and agony my father went through, unable to speak or control his body after sudden, multiple strokes stemming from previously undetected pancreatic cancer. And the suffering in my grandmother's voice when she pleaded with me at her nursing home: "I am too old!" I'll never forget my helplessness as my mother pulled me aside in fear and anger a few days before she died and gasped, "I can't stand this anymore!"

And so, I want to do this "right"—to figure out what "right" might be—because sometimes, I am just so fucking scared.

In a moment of numb anxiety, these words I wrote in "The Serpent Queen" came to my mind.

See?

She did see. She saw how beautiful the light was as it played through the trees, how elegant and perfect the hummingbird darting among the dark leaves and bright flowers. She heard the music of flowing water; the soft whispering of creatures moving through the shadows. There was living, and dying too, she understood, as each individual sprang forth, blossomed, then faded and merged into the greater harmony of all beings. Above all, she felt a vast contentment.

Maybe this passage is a clue to something I didn't realize I knew about myself? In the past weeks, I have spent long stretches of time sitting out on our porch or wandering up the logging trail into the woods. I don't remember ever seeing so many birds and animals: moose, fox, deer, rabbits, chipmunks, ground squirrels, a marmot (!) and, this morning, a lethally effective weasel; bluebirds, robins, hummingbirds, wood peewees, flycatchers, grosbeaks, wrens, chickadees, crows, ravens, woodpeckers, flickers, swallows. Because all the birds have recently had babies, the trees around me are filled with the stereophonic voices of bird parents and children calling to each other.

I am comforted to be a part of this web of life and death (let's not forget the weasel with jaws clenched on a dead mouse). I sit quietly or walk, and I listen. My mind travels back to myself as a child walking through the woods, anticipating meeting God and coming upon a deer instead, to the confused young woman standing on a precipice at the top of the Jungfrau, startled from her grief by a small bird landing at her feet whose sudden appearance dissuaded her from taking one more calamitous step, to the middle-aged woman kayaking alone on a lake where she perceived the world in front of her eyes parting while another glimmered just behind it.

I will stop before trying to interpret or draw conclusions. Like swimming underwater with the fish in Saint John, being surrounded by the many consciousnesses of different creatures soothes my fear and awakens happiness and curiosity in me. Sometimes, even a curiosity for whatever it is that comes next. On the porch, in my bathrobe, I observe and participate in this world of creatures. Maybe this is where I will find my answer to those "shoulds." I think back to the much-quoted last lines of "The Summer Day." Such a fiery exhortation! We almost forget what the poet herself has informed us she is doing on this day of her "one wild and precious life." She is simply observing a grasshopper munching on a piece of sugar.

It seems important to add a mention of my conversation with Alan this morning. Last night, I found myself crashing back and forth between guilt at my certainty at having ruined Alan's life and anger at this illness that often makes me feel so fearful, isolated, and dependent on him.

This morning, Alan said to me: "It seems as if so many bad things have happened. First, the pandemic, and then you being diagnosed with a brain tumor. And yet, because of COVID and my MS, I decided to retire early, and we've been able to spend more time together. Because of your diagnosis, we got rid of a second house we didn't need, and we've discovered how much we love it here. We've stopped worrying about putting things off. We don't act like other 'retired people' taking the required bucket-list vacations—we just do what we want.

"We sit at the dinner table or on the porch like two happy old people, and because of all that's happened, it feels like we're lucky— like it's more than enough. I know you thought you were supposed to take care of me. But as it turns out, you've given my life meaning because I get to take care of you."

It is difficult to imagine being worthy of this. But let's just say I felt so much lighter after our conversation, so much more able to release myself from the small, closed box of my fearful mind. I perceive possibilities I have, *now*, for happiness, love. For an extraordinary life.

Love,
C

July 15, 2023
New York, New York

I LOVE THE POEM "Joe Heller" by Kurt Vonnegut. It's Vonnegut's
description of an incident in the lives of these two gruff, visionary writers, whose words have electrified so many imaginations, but
who, at points, might still be dealing with twinges of inadequacy.
They're attending a party given by a billionaire neighbor out in the
Hamptons, and Vonnegut needles Heller by noting that their host
has made more money in a day than Heller made over the course of
his lifetime for his seminal novel, *Catch-22*. The poem records the end
of their exchange:

"And Joe said, "I've got something he can never have." And
I said, "What on earth could that be, Joe?" And Joe said,
"The knowledge that I've got enough."

For me, it's both an elegant acknowledgement of contentment
and a sort of tongue-in-cheek reminder not to take myself seriously.
It reminds me to focus on the shifting knowledge that I do, in fact,
have enough. And that the "shoulds" can go to hell.

I spent a wonderfully relaxed short holiday out in Amagansett with
Mom, Yannis, and Maria Alexia. The kids had to leave on July 4, so I
had two more days with Mom just to compare reading lists, walk on
the beach, laze around the backyard, and drink an entire pot of coffee
each morning as we discussed politics, the resurgence of reactionary

Catholicism in her parish, the nuances of gender identity and why pronouns matter (Mom's not convinced), and reminisced over old photographs. On my last day, I drove into East Hampton with Mom in the morning, left her at her volunteer job, and walked home, up Egypt Lane, across Middle Lane, and down to the beach at Two Mile Hollow. It was beastly hot and humid, so I yielded to temptation and walked down to the shoreline to dip my hands in the cold Atlantic and, maybe, rub them through my hair. Lulled by the freshness of the breeze off the water, I forgot the basic rule of never trusting the ocean, and was shocked, then amused, by the crash of a rogue wave that doused me from head to toe! I was sopping wet and still had about a mile and half to walk home, so I decided to enjoy it, and walked at the high tide line, carrying my shoes (which I had fortunately removed and left safely high in the sand when I went down to cool off).

That led me to the discovery of the day: a series of tiny, translucent opercula left behind by their whelk creators. Opercula are relatively rare and can be found only on certain mysterious days—I haven't been able to identify a lunar or other pattern to their appearance on the beach. They resemble tortoiseshell in color and have the whorl of the nautilus, which I believe is a Fibonacci sequence. (My math skills are no better than in tenth grade, when Mr. Conti pleaded with me to at least try to understand geometry. Never happened, but he had his revenge when I had to work with Greg, whose mathematical perception was even worse than my own, in attempting to understand how to calculate the volume of a cone.)

So, I got home, still damp but grinning with my haul of opercula. And I felt intensely, in that moment, that I had enough.

But life has a way of sneaking up on you, doesn't it? I stayed in the city this week, with various social events and a follow-up with the vitreo-retinal specialist, who was very pleased with the progress of the eye. (Doctors, as you may have noticed, don't telegraph their concerns until the danger has passed—it turns out that he had been worried about the sheer volume of blood in the eye and was relieved to see that it had been mostly absorbed.) Wednesday evening, I joined our high school classmate Claire for drinks and music at an Irish pub down in the East Village. The husband of one of her friends was playing in the band. Several other friends of Claire's were there as well, and we had a really enjoyable time talking about family, houses, and summer activities. Then, one of the women asked how many children I have. I answered, as I usually do, that I raised two but that my younger son had died by suicide. Their reaction was instantly empathetic and loving, but it was as though a switch had been thrown—the bar was suddenly too loud, the air conditioning too frigid, the evening lacking in meaning. I stayed for another twenty minutes or so, both hoping to get past the feeling and not wanting to cast a pall over these lovely women's evening, but everything was leaden. I eventually pleaded an early morning start (true) and said my goodbyes. The evening was cooling, the sky still lit and full of pink-purple clouds, and walking across 14th Street, I felt gratitude for this city seeping into my grief.

And work is therapy of the best kind. I've spent the last two days working in the north end of the park at the Dana Center. A massive cloudburst yesterday morning before I left for work cleared the atmosphere and dropped the temperature enough to allow me to walk there, about a mile and a half, smelling the petrichor and feeling the breeze off the Meer. We were short-staffed, so I was on my own at the desk for most of the day, but Fridays are slow; visitors linger and talk, and I chatted with children and tourists about fish, the park gates, blue-green algae, the reconstruction of the swimming pool—all the park-nerd things that give me joy.

There will always be moments of leaden absence, but for the most part, I have enough.

Love,

J

July 30, 2023
Breckenridge, Colorado

I HAVE COME TO THE same place—that same stretch of single track on Gold Hill where the dirt trail squeezes between clusters of small pine trees with wild pink roses tangled beneath them—when the thought that I'd had two days before in this very location occurs to me again. This time, I stop.

The experience is not exactly like the gathering of a thought. Instead, what appears in my mind is the impression of hearing a voice. Is it my voice? It announces: *I'm sorry. I'm sorry it has to be this way. But in the place of a very long life, you will have a blessed life. An extraordinary life.*

As I stand still, images come to mind. I think of my husband, the ease of our relationship, the joking, even the arguments that occasionally arise, falling back into the mostly placid ocean of our day-to-day patterns. I glimpse the two of us sitting together on the porch bench with our breakfasts: *The chickadee landed on my coffee cup just before you came out! I think I hear the wren. Look, there in the tall grass is the rabbit... Do you see it?* I smile at the strange wonder of how I am able, in quiet moments, to not just imagine but to *be* the person I was with him as a teenager, all heat and dreams.

I see our home, where inside the house and within paintings, hand-me-down furniture, well-thumbed books, and embroidered pillows live generations of my family. On the kitchen counter, my phone holds text messages from nieces and nephews: One niece is excited about the offer of a new job; my nephew is proud of good grades; and another niece wants to review the logistics of an adventurous trip to the Middle East. I am comforted to be surrounded by the tangible presence of all these people I love.

In the disorder of trees of all sizes and unkempt grasses around the house, among the bluebells, dandelion, and wild lupine, live so many wild creatures—maybe even generations of birds and animals. I like to think that many of the birds were once fledglings that launched themselves from the birdhouses Alan and I made. I hope other wild neighbors, like the fox and the moose and the shy, dusty garter snake, find peace and safety here.

Reading, thinking, and writing comprise much of my days now. All my life, it seems, I never gave myself permission to set aside the hours to do these things. Now, I give myself permission. And what's more, I receive back from this community—in which I have lived for ten years—interest and appreciation for this part of myself, something I'd never experienced before.

I've wandered around for so many decades of my adult life, looking for love, for time, and a safe space in which to be creative. For home. If my life is shorter than it might have been because of my illness, I will be sorry.

But today—right now—as I turn to continue this hike with the slow familiarity of walking meditation, I see clearly that there are many kinds of lives that might manifest for a person. In the end, all lives pass in a moment. Our days are barely longer than the rose, and sometimes shorter than the pine. And though none of us gets to choose our life, still, I would choose this one.

May we both experience the feeling of enough,
C

August 10, 2023
New York, New York

I AM COMING OFF A contentious phone call with my wasband—an argument spurred by his need to control, to gaslight, and to manipulate the narrative between us. We had a joint account at a bank that was being absorbed by another institution, and he rushed to withdraw any funds that might have been in his name. I had been using the account exclusively, and he knew (or should have known) that the funds in it were mine, but he was delighted to discover a $4,000 "windfall." I confronted him the very next day, after my debit card was refused twice, but instead of admitting his error, he demanded proof that the funds were mine. This was impossible since it would require access to the now-shuttered online banking facility of the defunct bank. He's been in banking for thirty years and knows this. He then presented a totally distorted narrative of events to somehow demonstrate that he "loved me more." I lost my temper and told him that if he loved me at all, he would win on that score because I did not have any love at all for him any longer. It was harsh and apparently devastating for him, although it's not the first time I've told him. I'm still fuming.

I'm glad you're feeling that you are a part of all that you touch—the people, the creatures, the lodge pole pines that stand stark and brave above the low bushes and flowers on the hills above your home.

I gave Yannis one half of the ammonite that I bought on a recent trip; the two polished surfaces are mirrors of one another. He and I bring each other little gifts from our trips now, something I hadn't done since he and his brother were little, and I would search for their Christmas ornament for the year—an embroidered Big Ben from London, a dancer from India, a kangaroo from Australia. I see echoes of these mementoes at so many points—carved wooden animals that remind me of the year the boys chose their own ornaments in Jackson Hole, Wyoming, on a family holiday in 2009 where my parents celebrated their fiftieth anniversary with their four children, respective spouses, and ten grandchildren. Dad and Greg are gone, and my ex has been removed from the picture—the twenty of us are down to seventeen, about to be augmented by one as my brother's oldest expects her first child in October.

I've had two magical weeks of work punctuated by visits to my mom. I was once again reminded that weirdness is hereditary—politics, family history, the succession of the Persian emperors, and how Zoroastrianism happened to migrate to India are some of the topics that have been volleyed back and forth over coffee. We hunt for the perfect beach rocks together (I prefer rounded, egg-smooth quartz pebbles, Mom has a weakness for gradations of color and cracked ones that sparkle), discuss shell preferences, and the fact that, as children, each of us thought collecting wampum would make us rich. I made her your spectacular almond cornbread and *kolokythokeftedes*, the Greek zucchini fritters that she swoons for; she found me a new bedside table in the donations at her organization and helped me strip the finish to reveal the wood, adding the final touch of a polishing wax she purchased about forty years ago with Dad and has hoarded for special occasions since then.

These are the moments that I have become attuned to cherish: time with my vibrant, interesting, loving mother, who is also my friend. We are protective of each other, a shift in the dynamic that has been slow but frictionless.

Other moments in the city are magical—seeing the mist rising off Conservatory Water after an intense downpour, leaving an evening concert at the band shell with Vivaldi still echoing, and walking out through the softly illuminated Bethesda Terrace to the waning light. And there will always be the moments that catch in my throat, like when a woman stopped me to comment on the message on the back of my sweatshirt. It says:

> Dear person behind me, the world is a better place with you in it. Love, the person in front of you.

She told me she lost her son to drug addiction; I told her I lost mine to suicide. She hugged me and looked me in the eye and said the devastating words I hear, so often, in my head: "We were supposed to protect them." Most of the time, I can answer, truthfully, "I did the best I could."

> Sometimes doing our best is really hard.
> Love,
> J

August 17, 2023
Breckenridge, Colorado

MY HEART ACHES AS SUMMERTIME comes to an end. Yes, these days will be transformed into the golden fall, the crystalline winter and, one day, raucous spring again. But this summer is gone. This one. In the sorrow I feel over the waning of these long sunny days, there is my stubborn refusal to accept change. Despite sixty-two years of observing the blooming and the fading, the cold and deep torpor, and then the rebirth, I am angry because summer must end. And so, I suffer.

August third arrived as another terrifying day during which I could not bear to think or stop myself from thinking: *What if the results of today's MRI are not good?* Thankfully, the scans showed "no tumor regrowth." But the stress had been so intense that Alan and I fought all the next two days. By the following Monday, like leaving a bad dream behind, I awoke without fear or anger. The sky over Peak One pulsed a strong and vibrating blue. We talked, cried a little. We returned to ourselves, and we got back into living.

A photographer in our county, with whom I was acquainted and had had some unpleasant business dealings, died last week. His death struck me hard. I got to thinking, during a walk on one cool morning, of how easy and justifiable it feels to cling to what we love—and equally, how easy and justifiable it feels to cling to what makes us angry.

Several years ago, I raised $35,000 to produce a book I was keen to work on with this well-recognized photographer. The money secured, he kicked me off the project, stating that, because of my work on a previous photographic book, he saw me as a competitor. For years after, I nursed my anger at him. Then, last year, I saw him seated, like me, in the UC Health Anschutz oncology department. I soon found out that, like me, he had been diagnosed with cancer.

During the following months, he would send me occasional messages: congratulations on the publication of my new novel, words of encouragement about my illness, and sometimes notes revealing his own physical pain and the failure of his treatment. His kindness surprised me and softened my heart. He wrote to me, and I wrote back, until five days before he died. We had become, if not friends, comrades on this hard journey.

I recently met my aunt again for a walk. I have approached these encounters hesitantly. Her harsh behavior toward my dying mother—her sister—remains painful to me, difficult to fathom, and transformed her into a stranger. But as time has gone by, as I have faced my own mortality, I have some idea of how grief can distort us.

During this hike around the reservoir near our house, we bushwhacked off the trail—as my family was always determined to do—pleased with ourselves for finding "the better route away from *people*." We concluded that we have both, in our older years, become like my grandparents in our crotchety dislike of crowds and of all things modern or with touch screens. Her eyes rimmed red with tears when she asked about my health. In this small, seventy-six-year-old woman I recognized family.

Finally, a surprise encounter with myself.

While visiting friends in Glenwood, I sat with my coffee after breakfast and admired their beautiful modern home. The matching furniture, the newly renovated kitchen, and the lovely framed, studio photographs of my friends with their son stood as evidence of their hard work and the success they have achieved in life. I thought of how they had gone from college to medical school to residency to practice; had married and had a child. Had become respected members of their community.

They had not strayed from the continuous path of accomplishment—*ever*—as far as I know. And in a wave of self-understanding that also felt without judgment, I saw clearly how I could never have lived that life. Even though, with its sense of order and security—safety—it was a life my family might have wished for me. A life that I, many times, might have wished for myself.

One afternoon decades ago, when I was on a printing assignment in Italy, I sat at a restaurant table in the courtyard of a fifteenth-century manor house. My Italian colleague sat across from me. It was autumn, and we drank small glasses of grappa under a persimmon tree laden with soft, orange fruit. Our conversation meandered among the subtleties of offset lithography: How to reproduce the blue of the heavens? Or Ferrari red? Soon, we'd return to the plant and the book we were printing. In a week or two, I'd be back in New York, hoping for another assignment so I could pay my rent.

This one afternoon beneath the persimmon tree stood in for all the experiences in places around the world, all the moments—some beautiful, some ill-advised—that have enriched my days and composed the life I really did want to live. I sat in my friends' house in Glenwood and acknowledged the goodness and contribution of their lives and felt at peace with my own.

About the photographer or my family or myself, I can't say that I no longer see the aspects that were so hurtful, cruel, haphazard. I can't say that I am now okay with bad or destructive behavior. The dark angles, the shadows are still there. But the picture has been filled in with shading and subtleties, allowing my feelings about the whole person—and about myself—to shift and move away from being stuck *all the time* in anger or self-doubt. Allowing me friendship, connection, self-acceptance.

With spring came the ecstatic energy of birds singing and building nests, growth and greenery everywhere I looked. Summer gave us warm mornings on the porch in which we noted with pleasure each new plant blooming in the garden. Now at the end of summer, there is more than a cool hint of fall. The marmot, deer, bluebirds, and even the insects are active in a different, more purposeful kind of way. They are not holding on to summer. They are accepting and preparing for change.

> In each new experience, another dimension of the soul unfolds.
> —John O'Donohue, *Anam Cara*

Love,
Chris

August 23, 2023
New York, New York

ACCEPTANCE—THAT'S A HARD ONE, isn't it? I'm still somewhere between rueful, embarrassed, and bemused with myself over my inability to get over the last interaction with my ex. I think it's behind me, and then I wake up playing out scenarios in my head, things I should have said to him, ways I could have devastated him verbally, made him understand why he was such an absolute shit and how self-servingly blind his justifications were. Then I remember the old adage about not playing chess with a pigeon: They aren't very good at it, but they don't care; they shit all over the board and walk away, and you can't really win. It's a lesson I am still absorbing. But I always find humor healing, and I have resorted to mental renditions of Audrey Hepburn railing at Rex Harrison in *My Fair Lady* when she sings, "Just you wait, Henry Higgins." I can enjoy the music and clever lyrics of Rogers and Hammerstein and make gentle fun of myself simultaneously.

My other antidote for unhealthy rumination is creativity. In December 2019, when we had already been separated for nearly three years, my ex had asked me to accompany him to a holiday gala which would be attended by many of our close friends, but I declined. I later found out that he brought his girlfriend, whose existence he had deliberately concealed from me. (Not Camilla, a woman he had found on Tinder, I think.) I had no issue with his having a girlfriend, who would have been the logical choice to bring anyway, but I was infuriated that he hadn't had the decency to tell me and embarrassed that I learned it from other people. My therapy was to take my wedding dress, which had been sitting in a box on top of our closet since 1995, to two couture buddies and have them deconstruct it, all while sipping wine and singing, "I'm gonna wash that man right out of my hair." It was one of those voluminous early-1990s dresses that looked like it escaped from *Dynasty*; my friend had long made fun of it in our wedding photo, joking that he could make me a dress out of the bow alone. That didn't happen, but I did get a dressy blouse, a bodice, and a pair of trousers from the dress, and a graffiti-covered, oversized shirt from the lining.

So, this episode of being pissed off inspired me to write a poem. In one of my wandering explorations of Instagram, I came across a poet named Joseph Fasano, who writes lovely, short, accessible but not dumb poems that remind me in many ways of our beloved Mary Oliver. In following him, I learned that he also creates poetry prompts to help people at various stages of life and literacy to express the inexpressible. Think of it as a sort of exploratory Mad Libs—they've been given to refugees, nonverbal autistic people, and other nontypical poets, with surprisingly beautiful results.

I once read a quote that purports to be from Sappho, but I haven't been able to find confirmation of it in any source, even among my ancient Greek poetry nerd posse, so I don't know what it would look like in Greek, but in English, it's "what cannot be said will be wept." The alternative to weeping, for me, is to sing it, a poetic threnody, I think. I reached out to Mr. Fasano and asked if he could come up with some prompts that might be useful for parents who've lost their children to suicide. He responded immediately with a prompt that was to be included in his upcoming book, and generously offered it for use by me and those in my bereavement group. This is the poem I came up with:

Poem by a Parent

My beloved Gregos, it took me so long to meet
the she-wolf inside me.
It took me so long to let the she-wolf inside me go.
Now that I can sing out like a swallow
I hope that you can hear
the joy you come from;
I hope you know that you are not a failure.
You are the luminous heart pulsing
in the universe.
You are the catch in my throat.
You are the Icarus that no one can contain.
What I mean is this: I love you.
If I were a swallow, I would sing for you.
If you were tired, I would let you nestle.
Grego mou, I will love and mourn and
celebrate you, until you find your peace.

Fasano's book, out soon, is *The Magic Words*—I've placed a pre-order.

My other creative adventure recently was making a Turkish glass mosaic lamp. I am the least artistically talented of my siblings—my older brother hand forges knives, as I've told you before, my sister is a talented artist in watercolor and acrylics, and my younger brother's woodworking talents extend from bowls and baseball bats to a fully functional, gorgeous surfboard of various hardwoods. I can wield a drill with the best of them and know how to replace washers, build Ikea furniture, and hang a shelf so that it's even, but I am flummoxed when it comes to creativity.

I am, however, really patient if I have a goal and a pattern. Back in early 2020, just before the pandemic got traction, I took part in a mosaic workshop run by a friend in Athens. I had a design—a nautilus shell—and a pile of marble bits in various sizes and colors. It was slow but meditative, and some twelve hours later, I had a lovely (and heavy!) piece of art. It now lives at Valeria's house.

So, I saw this advertisement for a glass mosaic workshop and signed up. I had bought a hanging version of one of these lamps in the Istanbul Grand Bazaar in about 2006, and it was installed in the staircase of the Agiannaki house. I remember choosing it, bargaining with the seller, and then getting my husband involved. My ex loved to bargain—a skill he had inherited from his mother, who invented the improbably perfect word *bargue* (rhymes with "argue") for her own unique style of alternately wheedling and arguing. A Turkish man will always treat another man with greater deference than he will a woman, and given my ex's tenacity and zeal, we did, in fact, get a bargain. I loved seeing the light filtered through the riot of colors, red, blue, green, and yellow, as I walked down the steps.

In the workshop, I once again proved adept at following a pattern and gluing things patiently. I was rewarded with a lovely little globe in the blue, turquoise, and green glass tiles of my choosing that now decorates a shelf in my living room. I feel as happy as a kid whose noodle collage decorates his mom's fridge.

This morning, as I was looking proudly at my newest décor item, I realized that it's also a connection to Greg and his ability to navigate the loud, chaotic, visually overloaded passages of the cavernous bazaar. Greg had an uncanny skill for remembering the twists and turns that would take us from Ugur, the dealer in "genuine fake watches," to the rug guy, to the sellers of spices and tea, to the shop that sold the best versions of high-quality knock-off handbags, including a credible version of the famous Hermès Birkin. (I used to take so many Greek women friends to this shop that the owners assumed I was a tour guide and offered me free bags as a kickback—I still have a decent-looking black "Louis Vuitton" evening clutch).

Greg loved the hubbub—the kid couldn't subtract twenty-seven from one hundred with any consistency, but his sense of direction was unerring.

Greg is also the reason for my latest Spotify obsession, an Indian woman bagpiper who combines versions of traditional sea shanties or Irish/Scottish music with Punjabi drums. Don't ask me why; it just works. The music reminds me of his joy and abandoned dancing at a pub in Killarney after a couple of pints. He just felt all emotions so deeply, including the breathless sense of *agalliasi* at music that moved him to his bones. I smile, sometimes through tears, as I listen and think of him.

Love,
J

August 26, 2023
Breckenridge, Colorado

I AM REALLY IN A terrible way, and I am going to lay this on you. This particularly awful period began when you made a comment the other day about how many of my pieces communicate the sense of shame I experienced growing up. Suddenly, that was all I could think about! And so many examples came shooting up to the surface of my mind.

From murky dreams and memories of inappropriate familial touching to some awful experience with neighborhood kids when my family had just moved into our house on Edgewood Road when I was five. Creepy babysitters: a sadistic old lady and even a teenage guy from Children's Village, an organization that helped troubled children. This kid was being fostered by a neighbor, and (is this possible?) my parents thought he'd be an acceptable babysitter. Oh yeah, and then there was the teenage girl across the street who threatened to stick an umbrella up my vagina. *Holy shit.*

A time-out: I am not blaming you for your observation. It's like all these examples were looking me right in the face, but I didn't see them for what they were.

In the midst of what I now see was a lot of chaos and scary shit for a young kid, my dad's parents were killed in a car accident. I lost two kindly grandparents I loved. And whatever protective impulses my father had, whatever interest he had in me—his eldest child who adored him—withered. He was emotionally traumatized; he withdrew, and the occasional attention he did spare for us was mostly of the angry, frustrated, violent kind—at least until we kids were all quite a bit older.

Once out of high school, I was invariably attracted to men who at first seemed extremely interested in me, almost obsessively, sexually so. I was always starving for attention. Then, that attention turned mean, jealous, or violent. Or to a kind of cruel, taunting indifference. So, sexual obsession turned to shame. The most stand-out example of this was my first husband. As I have noted, at one point, my entire family refused to speak to me for over a year as punishment, I suppose, for my transgression in marrying someone they despised so profoundly. The irony, of course, is that this isolation made it even harder for me to think clearly and find my way out of that horror show.

And I will jump ahead forty years, to today, to the last twenty-four hours in which Alan has refused to speak to me. Yesterday, we had a call with an insurance broker, as our medical insurance through COBRA is up at the end of December, and we will have to find individual insurance. She warned us that it would be expensive and that no matter how much we paid, we might not be able to see the same doctors or be treated at the same facilities.

I panicked. Alan's twice-yearly infusions for MS will likely not be affected—as these can be administered at almost any hospital. But the threat of losing my doctors is frankly terrifying. Alan tried to remain calm and to reassure me that we will find a way, that we have the means to make sure I get treated by the same doctors. But I know that without coverage, we are talking hundreds of thousands of dollars. We discussed buying a place in Denver so we could become Denver residents and eligible for a greater variety of insurance plans.

But I was, and am, really scared. And so angry. I feel ashamed that because of me and this cancer, I have thrown our lives into this kind of turmoil. That I am potentially going to cost us thousands and thousands of dollars.

Later, Alan and I went out to get some soup, and over a simple disagreement about what size soup to get, Alan completely lost it and went storming out of the restaurant. He wouldn't speak to me for the rest of the day. I tried to speak to him this morning, and all he would really say is that he can't take the constant sense of crisis anymore. And as I have so many times before in my life, I felt this bottomless well of fear at losing the love of the person I care about because of some shameful thing I have done—in this case, brought cancer into our lives.

This past week, we've received news of three people we know dying of cancer. And while I feel well, I can't stop thinking of my own prognosis. I think Alan is scared, too, and trying to control his emotions and the eruption of chaos in our lives with plans and busy-ness and lots of activity. But I don't know because he won't talk to me. And I am frightened. It's as if everything that ever terrified me in my life is making a return appearance. I am about as down as I have ever been.

C

Fall

September 6, 2023
New York, New York

OH, CHRIS. I'M SURE THINGS with Alan have resolved since you last wrote, but I'm so sorry you are dealing with such a cascade of fear, discovery, and difficult memories. I hope that, for you, writing has something of the cathartic effect it has for me. I used to compare it to the process of making Greek coffee, with the wait time required for the enjoyable part to clarify and the muck to settle to the bottom. Things are often muddled and swirling in my head, and by writing them down, they fit together in unexpected ways, but I'm almost always calmer. And if I can't sit and write, I go out and walk. That's how we started this whole project, isn't it? Walking, observing, and trying to explain it to someone else in order to have it make sense?

I've had a great balance of activities, busy days at work, really enjoying my colleagues as well as the visitors, except for the man who wanted me to mark on his map the location of every single water fountain in Central Park. On at least two Sundays per month, I take the 6.30 p.m. bus out to Amagansett, sailing against the summer traffic, to be embraced by my mother who's up past her bedtime and waiting impatiently at the stop in front of the Huntting Inn. This time, I brought her another loaf of your cornbread, which I made with mascarpone in place of the yogurt (no appreciable difference IMO), a new tea kettle (hers was leaking), and a white T-shirt I found at TJ Maxx that I knew she'd like. Yannis and Maria Alexia had been out for the weekend, returning to the city late Monday, so the four of us had some time together. I'm so happy to see the kids easy together, just comfortable, but very mindful that I can't get more invested in their relationship than they are, and that I have to tread a very thin line between acceptance and excess enthusiasm. And Yannis and Mom, who can strike sparks off one another, seem easy and less careful around one another too. It's a joy to have family together without having to watch where you step.

Our high school pal Desirée visited for lunch on Monday. She's rented a house in Cutchogue for a couple of weeks, and I became the sounding board for her own family Sturm und Drang. I'm always grateful for friends who listen and talk me off my emotional ledges, so I was happy to listen and offer the occasional insight. Families can be hard—tensions reverberate and ricochet off different players, with unexpected bruising and unexamined, but often carefully hoarded, resentments.

Examining these emotions made me all the more conscious over the next three days of how incredibly lucky I am to have the ease and emotional intimacy with my mom. We did a radical pruning of her sweet magnolia, which was starting to obscure light in the sitting room as well as provide a ladder to the roof for raccoons, and laughed ourselves silly stuffing all the cuttings into her car. We rewarded ourselves with fish tacos at Main Beach, where we watched the rain scudding across the sand, the lifeguard stand empty except for the stiffly blowing red flag, and the young guards milling about their break room in sweats and rain shells.

Mom is judicious about allowing me to do the things she wants to do but has thankfully become a bit more cautious about tasks like lifting heavy stuff and climbing ladders. Still, she's determined to do things her way. The "bump" on the top of her head turned out to be not just a basal cell cancer but a serious squamous cell cancer, and the Mohs surgery (that she had scheduled and gone to *alone* the previous week) was rather extensive. I was forbidden to mention it to my siblings but was allowed to help her clean the hair-raising suture lines. She has a consult with a radiologist this week—again, she'll go alone. I will follow up and threaten exposure to my siblings if she's not compliant with medical instructions. Yeesh.

You and Alan are now in Greece, and I look forward to regular dispatches. I can imagine that Athens was a reunion of mixed emotions—so much has happened since we met there five years ago, and I took you to places in Aghia Eirini, the "cool" district. You texted me that you stopped in Arachova on the way to Delphi and had a lovely experience. I'm so delighted that you loved Arachova, and honestly, being there in misty, rainy weather is probably more memorable than in relentless summer sun. I know I've told you something of my personal connection to this village, but probably not my experience at Barba Loukas's memorial service.

Arachova is a beautifully picturesque town perched on a vertiginous hillside, bisected by one narrow, winding main road through which all traffic to the Mount Parnassus ski resort and the World Heritage site of Delphi must pass. It also happens to be the ancestral village of my wasband on his mother's side.

My husband was named, against convention, for his maternal grandfather—the usual Greek practice is to name the first son for the father's father. As it happened, my father-in-law had been estranged from his own father (fortuitously, or he would have been baptized Kornelios), his maternal grandfather was apparently an absolutely saintly man and possibly the only positive male influence in his grandson's life. This grandfather's immediate family in Arachova was very poor, but he had an extended web of relatives of varying economic circumstances, and as a very young man, was offered the opportunity to leave the life of a barefoot shepherd boy and move to Piraeus to live with cousins. He left Arachova and prospered, and his life was radically different than the rest of the family's.

The Arachova connection stayed strong, though—my husband's mother spent many of her childhood summers with relatives there, and her son had developed a deep affection for one elderly great-uncle. Back in the early 1980s, Barba Loukas had been very welcoming and kind to the college-age crew who came to the falling-down family house high in the village, overlooking the clock tower, and stayed there while enjoying the newly introduced sport of skiing.

Barba is a village term of respectful affection that means "uncle," and metaphorically can mean "protector." I only met Barba Loukas once, during my first summer in Greece, when my Greek was still very shaky. I did not understand a single word he said. Part of this was due to the fact that he, like all Arachovites of his generation, eschewed the use of vowels and just strung consonants together and elided all his words; even other Greeks had a hard time working out what was being said. Add to this the fact that Barba Loukas had no more than four teeth and insisted on sharing his homemade "brusco" wine, which was the color of Tropical Fruit Hawaiian Punch and palatable only after multiple glasses, and I have no recollection of having ever understood what we talked about.

In January 1991, my mother-in-law received word from Arachova that Barba Loukas had died, and it was agreed that the three of us would attend his upcoming memorial service. Now, as you know, I am neither particularly tall nor particularly blonde, but by superannuated Arachovite standards, I was a blonde giant. (My mother-in-law was barely over five feet, so that didn't help.) I knew that I had to wear black, but I didn't think, in the frigid mountains in January, that I was expected to wear a skirt, and nobody told me until the morning of the service, when, of course, I had only brought black slacks. I stuffed them into my tall boots and hoped for the best.

We entered the church. There were smiles and whispered exchanges of hugs and kisses for the family, and frank stares for the "blonde giant" among the bent, black-clad old ladies. They were tough old birds—they all had some sort of shawl or cardigan over their black dresses, while I had on a heavy wool coat and could not stop shivering. The whispers began to intensify, but still, without vowels. After the umpteenth repetition (my Greek had improved by then), I was able to figure out that the essence of the exchange was the question, "Whose is she?"

Note that you have to belong—the question wasn't "who," but "who does she belong to?" And the identification was genealogical—the Arachovite who had left, and the following generations were identified by their relationship to him. Many years later, a local cousin explained to me that, at the turn of the century, the village still used patronyms more than surnames, and that many of the surnames currently in use were connected to professions. His family name, Milonas, means "miller," other cousins, "Economou," would have been the bookkeepers or accountants. The grandfather's surname, in contrast, was hilariously derived from an insult that basically means "lard ass."

So, now you know why I am so delighted that you loved Arachova, a place of family and history for me, and warm memories of a gentler time in my life.

> Have a wonderful trip.
> Love,
> J

September 20, 2023
Breckenridge, Colorado

W**E'D PLANNED A SAILING TRIP** in Greece back in April and
were so relieved when my August MRI showed good results
and allowed us to take this voyage. But arriving in Athens in early
September, we immediately felt your absence, Jane! Our friend, our
guide! You had helped us five years earlier to enjoy the most wonderful
honeymoon—showing us around the Plaka, taking us out to beautiful, wild Agiannaki to spend two weeks in your house on the beach.
All that set the tone for an easy-going exploration of the Peloponnese
and a deeply meaningful personal experience for Alan and me.

One memory of that time: driving from Athens to the beach
house. You pulled over on a quiet stretch of road. We all got out of our
cars, and you pointed to a trickle of a stream disappearing between
two rock walls. "Follow the stream," you told us, "see what you find."
And so we squeezed through the tight space, the stream deepening
and widening, and arrived at a pale blue pool beneath stony parapets
oozing with glittering minerals. High above, the space opened to the
soft movement of leaves, to the sky. We felt the magic of Greece, for
surely, in this place, gods and nymphs had once cavorted!

Our guide on this recent sailing voyage around the Saronic Islands
was a teacher of yoga and shamanism, in hindsight, perhaps a tip-
off as to why things didn't go as expected. I have known this teacher

for nearly fifteen years. The practice of yoga has continued to help me through difficult times, and its combination with shamanism—a willingness to consider a healing relationship with energy, dreams, spirit animals—has appealed to me. Ten years ago, I joined this teacher and a small group of students on a trip to the Sacred Valley in Peru and to Machu Picchu, a journey that was full of enchantment. We spent our days hiking through ancient ruins, meeting traditional healers, allowing ourselves as a group to fall under the spell of the great *Apus*—mountains that are the spiritual guardians of the Andes. But I realize now that I had always cut this charismatic man a lot of slack for his tendency toward exaggeration and for not following through on his word. These seemed like small irritations compared to all the good I'd experienced.

On this trip in September, we raced from port to port and, with few exceptions, were sent off in the direction of shopping and restaurants. My teacher's New Age vocabulary, which I'd once listened to with a mix of interest and indulgence, now seemed irritating and boastful. His wife, who joined us on the boat, added to the bluster by announcing that as a martial artist, she had had to "register her hands as deadly weapons."

Hearing this, I rolled my eyes, and Alan lost it, guffawing loudly.

But what was most disappointing was that the teacher had encouraged me to come on this expensive trip as a "healing journey," during which he and I would have plenty of opportunities to speak of spiritual matters. I looked forward to this as a way to let my mind wander and explore different pathways that might lead me to a greater understanding of my own mortality. But in the end, he never made time to have those conversations.

We had arrived in Greece a week before the sailing trip began. During this time, we drove from Athens to Arachova and the Temple of Delphi, and then to Kastraki and Meteora. In Delphi, mist rose up from the gorge during a pause in the pouring rain. Like smoke, it wound among the columns of the sacred temples. In Peru, I had visited a site called Moray, the "navel of the universe," and had a vision of my future. Here in Delphi, site of the omphalos or navel, I had no visions but felt an awareness of time—of *now*, but also of the movement of time.

I contemplated all those who had lived and died and journeyed here to ask questions of the oracle. Before I left for Greece, my family doctor, who has also become a close friend, had encouraged me to consider, "What if you didn't have to know?" Here in Delphi, I understood both the keen human desire "to know" and how knowing may or may not give us what we want and certainly not always what we expect. I could honor the desire to know and let go of the necessity of knowing. As this site attests, sooner or later, the lives of all those who needed to know come to an end. And all of us will pass into what is unknowable.

What was our Greece journey? Alan says he has been on the edge of anger and depression for months, and I know I am often wrestling with fear, depression. Were the storms that followed us around from Athens to Meteora and then bedeviled our sailing trip meant to distract us from our inner struggle? Or were they caused by it? Alan was gruff and challenging toward my teacher, our boat captain. In the end, I sat bored and distant among the people who had joined us, our friends. Petulant, I brooded: Please *won't someone say something* interesting? *Or are we all going to spend this time together giving tedious performances about who we would like others to believe we are?*

I could think of nothing to say to enliven conversation, to shift the energy. Then, Alan puked on the boat, which seemed to sum things up for the two of us.

Our hosts more or less dumped us back at the port of Piraeus a day earlier than publicized. Most of us made other sleeping arrangements. But one older woman passenger, Mary, a retired airline pilot, decided to stay for the night on the companion boat we had been sailing with. As it turned out, Thanos, the hefty, sardonic Greek captain of this second boat, decided to stay on board too.

Mary was last seen by one of our friends on the back of Thanos's motorcycle. The two captains—Mary and Thanos—had taken off toward Athens for a night of bar hopping. That made me smile, to know that they had found their bit of magic.

Reluctantly seeing the humor in all of this,
Chris

October 17, 2023
New York, New York

WHAT IF YOU DIDN'T HAVE to know? And what do you do with the things you can't escape knowing? Your visit to Delphi, the Castalian spring, and the question of the value of oracles, or what we know, has set me to musing.

October, for me now, builds to a slow, inexorable point of—is it tension? Pain? Release from the pent-up anticipation of this terrible anniversary? I don't know. But October 21 is the day, three years ago, when Greg ended his life, soaring from a place that brought him peace, seeking, as he wrote, liberation rather than salvation. My own Icarus, his demise enabled by the very wings I had worked so hard to build him from the time he was a beautiful but nearly mute four-year-old, seemingly oblivious to the world outside his own head.

I spent years hunting down the best therapies, behavioral analysis, speech therapy, hippotherapy, classroom shadows when this wasn't done in Greece, psychological support, dyslexia-based reading comprehension specialists, constantly searching for ways to improve his chances of being able to function on his own as a happy, autonomous adult when I would no longer be there to protect him. And he learned to flex his wings and revel in their strength—but also to use them in ways I could not have imagined.

And I honestly don't think I could have done otherwise, even if I had known in advance. There is a stunning bronze in the British exhibition at the Met depicting the sea goddess Thetis, mother of the hero Achilles, in deep mourning as she brings him the armor she has had Hephaestus forge for him. Mythology tells us that she dipped the infant Achilles in the Styx to make him invulnerable to weapons—except for his heel. Thetis also knew of the prophecy that Achilles was destined to have either a short and glorious life or a long and peaceful one where his name would die out soon after him. Once he chose the short but glorious option, her only choice was to try to keep him alive as long as she could and to burnish his glory by giving him a suit of armor made by a god.

I certainly did not have any of Thetis' foreknowledge, but I can identify with her sense of helplessness. Could I have kept Greg dependent on me or on a guardian, unable to speak or read or think for himself? Would I have tethered him to keep him safe? His was such a brilliant, unorthodox mind. One of his classmates in philosophy at university told me that when Greg raised his hand, the other students were silent. They knew that, due to his stutter, it would take him time and tremendous effort to say what he wanted to say, and that he would express a view that none of them had ever considered.

I've talked with you a bit about the concept of characterizing people through the prism of whether they are illuminated from within (*autofotos*/αυτόφωτος) or are lit by the light of others (*eterofotos*/ετερόφωτος).

Among the self-illuminated, there is a very rare category of persons who are both utterly brilliant and utterly original, illuminated from within with a blazing light. But there are others, and I believe Greg was among them, whose light is smaller but still entirely their own. They do not seek to light the world but carve an original, odd, quirky path and are unfailingly kind to anyone seeking illumination. They also suffer from an isolation that can be terribly hard.

Those illuminated by the light of others, the *eterofotoi*, include most of humankind. If I were forced to fit myself into one or the other category, I think I must belong to those who reflect the light of greater minds, but in such a way as to maximize illumination, in the way that the glass prisms of a lighthouse spread a distant beam. I feel that I belong to the introverts, the observers, people more inclined to deflect attention than to seek it. The debilitating loss of my son has engendered an urge toward kindness and gentleness, which has become the motivating force behind my interactions—except with my ex. Oh well.

Of course, the majority of people fall into the larger category of the *eterofotoi* (sorry for the confusing plural ending; Greek grammar is very organized but bewildering to the uninitiated). This is the large, seething, dispiriting mass of those who are warmed by the reflection of anyone who displays more certainty than they and who judge their worth by how many bask in their reflected light. These are the ones Yeats describes in the poem "The Second Coming," who are full of passionate intensity.

The point of my ruminations, I suppose, is not that we can choose, necessarily, which category we belong to. But I believe we can choose not to join the last category, not to feed on the adulation of the weak, not to feed on adulation at all. Just to shine, honestly, with whatever light we possess. And to derive joy from the meteors, those who blaze generously and profligately, just for the beauty of it.

But back to oracles, and knowing, and whether the old gods have withered for lack of worship, or whether we can no longer hear the whispers of the Castalian spring because we have failed to offer the necessary reverence. Does it matter in the end?

I love the story of Julian the Apostate, the last of the Byzantine or Eastern Roman emperors who tried to withstand the inexorable march of Christianity. In Greek, his epithet is "Paravatis" or "Transgressor," indicating that his great sin was that he tried to overturn his uncle Constantine the Great's embrace of Christianity and return the empire to a cleaner, less corrupt, neo-Platonic ethical basis.

Constantine the Great, the first Christian emperor, was reputedly baptized on his deathbed so as to avoid dying in sin but spent his waning years brutally slaughtering most of his potential successors, including (I believe) two of his own sons. Julian was raised as a Christian and lived under the constant shadow of the dynastic sword falling on his own neck, but somewhere along the line, he had a tutor who instructed him in older writings. Julian died in 363 CE, after only a few years as emperor; Constantine's later heirs continued both his bloodstained path and his support for Christianity. Julian is remembered as a sort of quixotic outcast, a romantic, the last great hope for the old ways.

After acceding to the imperial throne following impressive military successes and the convenient demise of his cousin (who was also his rival and predecessor), Julian sought to revitalize the worship of the Olympian gods, and where better to seek their support than the oracle at Delphi? He sent an emissary to determine whether the gods still survived. His messenger's response is recorded in the ecclesiastical records of Philostorgius the Arian, who died around 426 CE, and whose works survive through the ninth-century reference of Photius in the Myriobiblion. A fairly clear translation is:

> Tell the emperor that the Daidalic hall has fallen. No longer does Phoebus have his chamber, nor mantic laurel, nor prophetic spring, and the speaking water has been silenced.

It's gorgeous and tragic in its simplicity and poignant finality.

So where do we go next when the gods fall silent, and the guidance we have sought can't be found? Maybe our doubt in the power of the divine has shaken its power; maybe, as often happens with the gods, their desires are fickle and obscure. I don't know.

All I know is that I can find moments of sudden joy where I did not expect it, and the emotion that most suffuses my soul these days is gratitude for what my son taught me. I watched him achieve milestones in his own way, painstakingly, idiosyncratically. It taught me to savor the smallest of steps forward and to measure less in terms of victories and more in progress.

And Greg taught me to see things through the eyes of others. A week or so ago, I had dropped off a book for a colleague who was working at the Castle , then wandered off into the Ramble. There's a new rustic bench built by conservancy staff, replicating one designed by Vaux and Olmsted, and it makes me smile. I wandered farther down to the waterfall designed by Olmsted that replicates a Catskills landscape painted by Frederic Church. Olmsted and Vaux exercised their imagination and vision with a splendid and profligate disregard for the exigencies of a budget—all their ideas were outsized and aspirational.

It was a rare moment of quiet and calm at this usually very popular spot. As I walked up the steps carved into the bedrock beside the waterfall, my only companion was a rat. I yelled at him, and he scurried back into his hole but then poked his silky brown head out and gave me the most reproachful look. I considered his little face—he looked more like a woodland creature that had a better claim on the landscape than I did and less like a classic New York rat who probably smokes Marlboros and carries a knife. I apologized to the rat.

It continues to amaze me at odd moments that I feel so at home in Manhattan and that Greece seems so far away. Then I read a quote from Beryl Markham's autobiography that seemed to sum things up perfectly:

> I have learned that if you must leave a place that you have lived in and loved and where all your yesteryears are buried deep, leave it any way except a slow way, leave it the fastest way you can. Never turn back and never believe that an hour you remember is a better hour because it is dead.

I read *West with the Night* some years ago when I was still living in Athens, when not having a key to my house at Agiannaki would have been unthinkable. It resonates so differently now.

Much love,

J

October 25, 2023
Breckenridge, Colorado

THE LIGHT IN ME, THE light in you—your thoughts on the light we carry or reflect made me think of an argument I had with a family member over the greeting *namaste*. I was living in Florida and teaching yoga after my second divorce. Some members of my family sympathized with the cohort of Florida parents intent on banning the practice of yoga in local public schools. This kiddy yoga amounted to a few moments of stretching and then sitting quietly and often concluded with the word *namaste*. The practice had been introduced as a solution to help calm the little restless beasts in between classes. As fundamentalist Christians, the parents asserted that the greeting, in particular, was sinful and violated their beliefs.

The salutation *namaste*, often spoken at the beginning or ending of a yoga practice with palms together at the heart, translates from the Hindu to something like: "The divine in me bows to the divine in you." This is sometimes also interpreted or spoken aloud as "The light in me bows to the light in you." To me, it is a moment of recognition that, despite our differences, on some level, we are the same and, therefore, must honor each other and the unknowable source from which we all spring. From that source, we each are granted a tiny spark of light, our connection to the divine fire and to each other.

But according to fundamentalist Christianity, the idea that an individual might hold a tiny spark of the divine is fiercely denied. It conflicts with the notion that human beings are sinners and by our sinful nature cut off from the divine, stumbling in the dark without light. Through various rituals and prayers and elimination of people and practices with which we disagree, the best we can hope for is to glimpse this light from afar. I cannot accept such a grim belief.

Speaking of the divine, I would like to offer up this poem, written during our trip to Greece. Now that the disappointment with the sailing trip recedes in my mind, the memory of this white staircase leading to the sky remains:

The Island of Poros
I push open the blue hotel shutters.
A narrow stone staircase cascades
from around a high corner
in white painted steps. Higher still,
an outcropping of red earth and stone
balances pine trees, fruiting cacti.

A church bell rings, once.
The long ladder of one-step-
after-the-next descends
to the winding side street below.

This morning I follow this street to another
set of steps leading down to the port.
The channel of blue sea tossed with foam
carries yachts and sailboats
and a sleek black ferry from Athens.

Passengers pour out
in a thick mass
as if squeezed
from a tube.

The pulsing energy of their complicated
plans—What to see? Do? Eat? Drink?—
roils across the dockside. They will go
to the beach, they will stay awake all night
laughing and shouting at one another.
People shove their way forward
onto the quay.

Later, back on the balcony of my hotel,
I watch as one person steps down the long
white staircase. After some time,
another. Each monkishly quiet.

A dish clatters, a soft
muffled sound behind thick walls.
An orange cat sits, alert
on one of the narrow steps.

Today when the sun shines over the clock tower
I want to climb that white staircase to the top.
I have some questions for the sky,

the sea. When the poet Elytis
gazed out at the ocean
he exclaimed, "My God,
how much blue you spend
so we cannot see you!"

A few words about our trip to Maine, which followed our return from
Greece. We swam in the end-of-September frigid waters of the pond,
rode bikes along the carriage trails, ate delicious seafood, and drank at
least one (well, maybe three) martini(s) during those ten days. Dreamy

and taking pleasure in each day as it unfolded, I was captivated by the softness of light, the fading reds and golds of leaves, deer grazing in the field outside the cabin, and the quietness and deep peace of this place.

Near the end of our time in Seal Cove, Alan and I walked down toward the pond, and with some trepidation, I pointed out the spot—an open mossy rise above the path, beneath a very old tree and with a good view of the pond—where I would like to have my ashes spread when I die. I would also like to have some kind of a marker stone placed there.

It felt as if we were under some sort of a lovely, comforting spell—it wasn't at all sad—Alan looked around and said, "Yes, it is so beautiful here, so peaceful." I asked if he thought he would like to end up in this place, too, one day, and he said yes. We also agreed that Luke's ashes should join ours, which made us laugh; we would all be together in the end. We went for one last swim in Seal Cove Pond, and I felt as if something very important that had been bothering me for a long time was at last settled.

Sending love to you and a wish for peace and healing as you remember Greg's singular light,

Chris

October 27, 2023
New York, New York

THE ANNIVERSARY OF GREG'S DEATH was the seventh rainy Saturday in a row in New York. It didn't affect me all that much because I'm working indoors on Saturdays anyway, and unless the rain is truly torrential, I've learned to dress for it and carry an umbrella. (The one exception was the day in September when two and a half inches of rain fell within an hour; the governor declared a state of emergency, and one of the Central Park Zoo sea lions floated out of her enclosure and explored the flooded park.)

This past Saturday, I was happy to have the meteorological mood as subdued and melancholy as I felt. I listened to Greek music and the bagpiper's threnody on my way to work. I had asked specifically to be assigned to the quiet Dana Center, and my wonderful boss was quick to grant the request.

I found myself sifting through the best of my memories with Greg, from the time he was a little boy through our last evening together. Greg had a unique ability to fall sound asleep under any circumstances when he was tired. When he was five, I had to remove his face from a plate of spaghetti where he had nestled on the pasta like a pillow, and then wrestled with trying to get pajamas on his totally unresponsive body; it was like trying to dress a squid. He kept this talent into his early teens—he never fussed or got cranky, just went to ground and stayed asleep through transfers up and down stairs, off and on buses, through concerts and general hubbub.

We had traveled with friends to Egypt for Easter 2004 and attended the Good Friday service in the sixth-century church of Saint Catherine in the Sinai. It's an extraordinary place—I put my hand on the twenty-foot-high cedar entrance doors, then noticed the sign—"Gift of the Emperor Justinian." Holy shit.

The Good Friday service is always one of the most moving of the year and probably the only time Greeks sort of behave in church. It was especially moving there, in this ancient outpost in the middle of a hostile and unforgiving desert, protected by high walls and a fatwa bearing the hand of Mohammed himself. The reenactment of the death of Jesus and his interment in the tomb is bleak but poetic— once more, I was reminded that the central message of Orthodoxy is that the finality of death is overcome.

The church is dimly lit by dozens of ostrich egg lamps (they've been electrified, a concession to the times). It had been a hot day; we all held small, brown tapers, and the chanting was soporific even to the most caffeinated among us. Greg, just six, turned to me to be picked up (there were no seats), and promptly fell sound asleep.

A sleeping six-year-old is a dead weight, especially when facing another hour or so of liturgy. I began edging around to the walls, looking for a place to lean at least. I spotted a set of circular stairs winding around a column, leading to a pulpit that wasn't in use— the lowest accessible step was occupied by a nun in habit. She looked ascetic, dry, austere. But I caught her eye in a mute plea, the corners of her mouth softened, and she shifted slightly so I could share a portion of her step. I sank gratefully to a seat on about a quarter of my butt. She checked to make sure I knew the liturgical responses in Greek and made the sign of the cross in the Orthodox manner, not the Catholic one. I passed scrutiny.

About half an hour later (it felt like more, the way a Wagnerian opera lasts a couple of hours but feels like it's been days), a family of three, father, mother, and young girl, approached my savior nun with happy smiles. I watched in wonder as her face transformed with light, joy, and generosity—it appeared that she was the young girl's godmother because she conjured out of her robes the traditional Easter gifts to a godchild, new shoes and a fancy decorated Easter candle.

A few hours later, I was trudging in darkness up the precipitous slopes of Mount Sinai to greet the dawn, to see what Moses saw. I thought about the metamorphic power of love, how this woman who had never given birth (and may well had never even had sex) was another being entirely with her spiritual child. And how Greg's singular talent had allowed me to witness a small Easter miracle.

My next-to-last memory with Greg came the night before I was due to fly to the US for three weeks, in October 2020, eager to see Yannis and my mother. The pandemic intensified my longing for the people I loved, and I took advantage of having both an American and a European passport to travel, swathed in masks and coated in antibacterial hand sanitizer. Greg asked me if I wanted to watch a movie with him. This was rare, as he usually watched various anime and Pokémon videos on his laptop in one room while I read or watched something else on TV in another. So, of course, I said yes.

The movie was *The Secret of Roan Inish*, a nineties film, sort of fantasy, about an Irish family forced to leave their island home and move to the mainland, who suffer a series of setbacks, the worst of which is the loss of a baby son whose cradle is lifted by the tides and lost at sea. Then, the boy's plucky older sister decides to return to the island and restore the family homestead, enabled by the mysterious assistance of the seals that inhabit the waters. There's a suggestion of her being a selkie, but I honestly don't remember all the details, just the shock of realization, returning for Greg's funeral, that he was trying to send me a message of comfort, that somehow, he would always be with me.

Yannis was off on Saturday, and as he had done the previous year, he rented a car and drove out to Montauk Point by the lighthouse, a place where the boys had often played and skipped rocks in the summers when we came to visit our American family. As he got there, close to sunset, he spotted a lone seal swimming right off the Point, cavorting lazily in the waves. Was it Greg? Chance? I believe that there are worlds connected in ways I cannot perceive.

The last words I ever said to Greg in person, as he hugged me and sent me off to the airport the next morning, were, "I love you, I'm proud of you, and don't hesitate to ask for help." And for that, I am grateful.

As the day wound to a close, there was one more activity I was determined to experience. For the first time ever, an art collective had been given permission to fly one thousand drones over the lake in Central Park in a coordinated light show. I went with Lucy and her husband, Trey, both giving me warm hugs that spoke eloquently of friendship and understanding.

It was magical. Thousands of people (I think the estimates were ten thousand) were packed cheek-by-jowl above Bethesda Terrace, jockeying for a clear view over the lake. The announced time of seven p.m. passed; the crowd grew restive. Then, suddenly and silently, a swarm of shimmering blue, then purple, wafted high in the sky, shifting direction like a flock of starlings or very disciplined fireflies. A collective exhalation of wonder—"Oooooh!"—escaped the crowd.

It was brief, less than ten minutes, but, as someone behind me remarked, better than fireworks. There was something eerie and powerful in the silent energy that made ten thousand jaded New Yorkers collectively gasp in delight. I thought of my boy and his lesson to celebrate with unrestrained joy in the beauty of the unexpected.

Love,

J

October 31, 2023
Breckenridge, Colorado

THE WANING MOON HAS GLOWED intensely these past few nights, and the reflection of moonlight off all the snow we've received is so bright that it almost looks like morning outside our window. Up the slope of Gold Hill where our house sits, across the Ten Mile Range, even in the arms of pine trees swathed in blankets of snow, the bluish light from the moon glows and creates this weird sense of an alternate daytime.

It's six in the moring now; I've been awake for a while, so I read your piece about Greg again and was moved and heartbroken by your reflections. I was also struck by the intentionality of your honoring him and mourning the brevity of his brilliant, intense life. Your words were a good reminder to me that gathering the forces of intentionality—creating a sense of purpose or meaning—can help us resist a complete surrender to despair. To witness and give our attention to the good, the beautiful, the miraculous, and the gift that is this short life.

I need to gather around me some of that intentionality—or should I say, pull myself together.

It seems to me that during the months of spring, summer, and fall, I was very often able to find some kind of peace with my health, my life. I paid attention to feeling physically well, I soaked up the beauty of mountain life with all the birds and animals and luscious growth due to this year's rain, and I spent time with friends. I won two book awards in the spring, and that certainly buoyed my spirits! My sense of purpose and optimism faltered during our September sailing trip to Greece, but thinking about it and writing about it, I was able to find some meaning—and humor—in all the mishaps.

Last Friday, we received a foot of snow and with that, any lingering whispers of summer and fall were silenced. I immediately became sluggish and nearly stupefied with depression. The sudden onslaught of winter (and negative temperatures) felt like death, and panic began to burble up in me: *I am not going to make it.* Then, about a week ago, right after I sent you my last entry, a few things happened.

Since the end of summer, August maybe, I'd have this brief thought that I should check the Facebook page of a very old acquaintance, a French man who was my boyfriend when we were both twenty, and I was studying in France.

Years later, we were each one of the other's dozens of Facebook friends, and I received an occasional message from him, usually a birthday or Christmas greeting. Now, for some reason, he was on my mind. So, a week ago, I checked his Facebook page and was so very saddened to discover he had died this past summer of a heart attack. In the early hours of the next morning, I woke up and said a prayer for him. I was facing the window, and in that moment, a shooting star zipped across the sky.

Forty-two years ago, we had this lovely romantic relationship that lasted the few months I was in Nantes. This has always been a wonderful memory for me because he was a nice guy (unlike many subsequent boyfriends) and because of who I was at the time too: young and strong, optimistic, very full of myself and my potential, ready to take on the world. His passing is another reminder to me of what is still so hard to comprehend: that each life is filled with incredible and improbable beauty while, at the same time, everything—everything—comes to an end: youth, strength, potential, and finally, this very existence of ours.

We hosted some friends at our house this past weekend. He is an Ivy League graduate and professor of law; she was a reporter and suffers from some illness which is undefined but may be early-stage myeloma. During this three-day weekend, the conversation was dominated by our friends' struggles wandering through the maze of contradiction that is illness: the importance of seeing only the best doctors at Stanford and Dana Farber, followed by the suspicion that these individuals may be callous jerks who have no time for you, *but* still you see them because they are "the best." The confusion our friends felt when confronted with disjointed treatment plans, the vagaries of pain and pain medication centers, the invasiveness of medical questionnaires, and how often during the day (*the day?*) to change one's protective face mask.

Some weeks back, we both pondered the question: What if you didn't have to know? In the past week, one person from my past has died suddenly of a heart attack. I must assume he lived his life and did not "know" that its end was coming so soon. On the other hand, these friends of ours have spent so much of their recent relatively healthy lives hunkered down and frightened before the possibility that illness and death may strike at any moment.

What if we didn't have to know? What if we lived both intentionally and with an acceptance that we *can't know*?

Well, I suppose that would lead me to take a deep breath, acknowledge once again that I don't know and can't know how long my life will be ... However, what I do know is that winter is around the corner. I can be intentional about winter, at least. Pulling out the long underwear, ski pants, and boots, reminding myself that, in fact, I do like to cross-country ski and to snowshoe and that I have even, optimistically, bought a limited downhill ski pass for this winter. There are neighbors I can call to walk with me. I have started another piece of fiction (which, right now, is a little gloomy), and we saw all four moose this morning, heading for the aspen grove.

And when I get my shit together and get dressed this morning, if I walk out on the porch, there is a good chance that a chickadee will land on my head.

I'll see you soon in Saint John! (And put off winter just a little bit longer).

Hugs,
Chris

November 13, 2023
New York, New York

M Y BAG IS ALMOST PACKED! I am so looking forward to seeing you and Alan in one of the places that you love—and being on the beach is a pretty good incentive too.

I am in a buoyant mood this morning, for several reasons. One, which I trust will make you smile, is that I had a very successful outing to Ace Hardware, exiting with three things I had intended to buy (toilet bowl cleaner, dishwasher tablets, and a small clay pot for transplanting my oregano) and two impulse purchases (a mesh colander and new boot laces). I also ordered a turkey for Thanksgiving (not from Ace, I hasten to clarify) and thought about how different this November is from last year. And how grateful I am for that. I was dressed for the cold—it was in the mid-thirties—and I also realized that this will be my fourth winter in New York. I now feel fully a part of this city, which both amazes and delights me.

I had a wonderful birthday—I went to an exhibition I had wanted to see, took part in the monthly Zoom call that Mary still organizes, went for a long walk and catch-up with Lucy, then took Yannis and Maria Alexia out to dinner at Delmonico's. I had learned from some podcast that Delmonico's was the first restaurant in New York to accept reservations from women in their own names, and decided this was the place to celebrate. I also sent out an email invitation to my Greek women friends to meet me in March at a resort owned by another friend and was greeted with an immediate positive response.

The best gift I received, though, was the night before, when my son called me just to tell me about a minor achievement that had made him happy. The past several years have been so full of grief and pain that most calls are either checking in on each other ("How're you doing?") or my listening to him vent about something that had made him unhappy. That he would call me just to tell me that he had conquered a very difficult course at his climbing gym and was happy was wonderful.

I think part of the buoyancy is also attributable to the fact that my mom stayed over Friday night on her way to a funeral in New Jersey, Saturday morning, and that I was working at the Dana Center all weekend. The days were crystalline, the fall colors on the trees were gorgeous, and Greg's tree is just outside the Conservatory Garden, so I can walk by and smile at it on my way.

The Dana gets moms with kids, grandparents out with their little ones, birders, budding fishermen (catch and release is permitted), people in search of a public restroom, and the occasional, mostly gentle eccentric. I always engage these folks in conversation as long as it doesn't stray too far into delusion, and I love to dish up obscure park facts, so the eccentrics remember me and greet me enthusiastically by name. This past Saturday, a new character showed up and stayed for several hours; he would retreat into the display room when other visitors came in, then , when the center was quiet, come back to the front desk to talk with me about trees, Napoleon's campaign in Egypt, the challenges of Black manhood, and his relationships with his adult children. It came out that he'd spent about twenty years in prison for drug-related offenses, and I suspect he was still struggling with some level of addiction (his hands trembled noticeably toward the end of the day), but he was curious, thoughtful, and clearly surprised that his presence was tolerated. I felt both glad and obscurely embarrassed when he thanked me for talking with him; I got the impression that it didn't happen much.

We all need connection, don't we? To feel heard, useful, remembered, and celebrated. As I prepared the invitation and started to list names, I realized that there were about thirty-five women in Greece whom I really wanted to see, and almost all responded with the same level of warmth and enthusiasm for seeing me. Connection is also what I treasure about working in the park—my colleagues are wonderful, there are multiple interactions daily with patrons of all stripes, and I get to go home and decompress surrounded by photos and mementos of a full, rich life. I get to come see you and Alan in a beautiful place and meet other people who love you. Last Thanksgiving was just me, Yannis, and my mom, lovely but too small for a turkey—this year, I've ordered a turkey that should feed about fifteen people. (Now, if only Yannis's invitees, by and large expat Greeks, could confirm that they're planning to come . . .)

And we have been writing for a year! What started as a mutual impulse to rescue one another from being crushed beneath landslides of grief has turned into a meditation on nature, acceptance, reverence, paying attention, and seeking joy. And a wonderfully affirming testament to women's friendships.

See you soon,

J

November 20, 2023
Saint John, USVI

W E ARRIVED IN SAINT JOHN about a week before you were due
to join us.

During this first week, we stayed in a house on a cliff-top, overlooking a quiet cove just east of Haulover Bay. In this past year, I have
developed an obsession with returning to the ocean—to see its movement and color, to hear its rhythmic pulse. Both Alan and I love to
enter that blue universe of water and mingle with its otherworldly
denizens. To be honest, as each of us has an illness that we can predict
will either kill us or severely limit us physically, we don't hold back
from throwing time or money at another trip to Saint John.

And yet, during this first week, everything seemed wrong. We
were at the tail end of hurricane season, and many of the house windows had been secured with shutters that could not be removed. The
house was perpetually too hot; several old air-conditioners made
such a racket that the noise overwhelmed the sounds of the sea, of
birds. Seasonal rains seemed to have contaminated the cistern, and
Alan and I got the runs. Bugs (a *lot* of bugs) were everywhere, and I
made myself nuts trying to *save the bugs!* and relocate them outside
the house.

My expectations were so high for this escape from "our real life."
And one morning, despite my good fortune at being in this beautiful,
beautiful place, I was so miserable that I went outside, sat down on
the stone wall in front of the house, and began to weep.

It was an anniversary of sorts, I realized. One year ago, I wrote that first letter to you, about sandhill cranes, about grief. One year ago, I spent nearly every waking minute of every day in fear.

Remembering with sudden clarity what those awful days had been like while sitting on a stone wall above the ocean surprised me, sparked curiosity even. Back then, the level of terror that had taken hold of me made it nearly impossible to experience my life, my surroundings, or small everyday things. Now, I stopped bawling and experimented with opening myself up . . . to myself. To my disappointment over the lack of niceties in this house—no coffee filters, or island spices, or half-opened bottles of interesting liquors! The sheets had holes, and the air-conditioning didn't work! *Okay, so I am petty and imperfect at times.* Next, I considered my fear of abandonment: Today, I had stayed behind while Alan and some friends went snorkeling. "All the healthy people," part of me whispered. *Let it go, you know you really wanted to be left alone.* Finally, I kept having nagging, dreadful fantasies about what it might be like to fall over the edge of the cliff—how quickly would death come? *Of course, I think about death. Accept it.*

I could smell the blossoms from the jasmine tree I was seated under. Yesterday's blossoms lay spent on the ground; today's were giving off a heavy, seductive scent. Tomorrow, there will be new blossoms. This is what is true. This is what I will remember.

The jasmine, yes, and also an extremely large, green, black, and gold iguana who had been hanging out in a tree at the side of the house in the past few days. I got up from the stone wall, and as I made my way around to the front porch overlooking the ocean, we both saw each other unexpectedly and started. But we had seen each other before. At our first encounter, this dragon-like creature had leapt in apparent terror *of me*, from the same branch he clung to now—falling down, down, down through leaves and branches and finally, landing in the brush by the beach.

But today, well, this particular monster and I had gotten used to each other. Learned to tolerate each other's presence. *Oh, it's you again*, we both said silently to the other. *So ugly and so beautiful. So strange and so familiar.*

The next week, it was time to celebrate your arrival (and a belated birthday!). We would be together! In the Virgin Islands! We would get schnockered on rum cocktails! *Way to go, us!*

As you know, I love the house we stayed at in Cruz Bay, not least of all because it feels cared for by the owner, which in turn makes me, as a guest, feel cared for. I love listening to the waves from bed, as I am sure you did from your balconied room, and gazing out at that view of the ocean that goes on and on until it disappears beyond the horizon. How amazing to see you, to see us both together—we two, once the goofy and extremely unlikely co-captains of the high school JV field hockey team—in this most unlikely of places!

Some memorable moments from our very memorable few days together (Alan and me, you, another girlfriend and her husband, and one of Alan's friends): You and Alan's friend arriving together on the ferry from Saint Thomas—it was not a surprise that even though you two had never met, he had immediately spotted you at the ferry terminal, perceived your confidence in navigating taxis and ferries in faraway places, and clung to you like a bug. You and I bobbed in the water while my girlfriend took our photo, and we instructed her to make sure all double chins and exposed bellies were not in the frame. You asking Alan, "What are you saying that is making Chris laugh like that?"

I loved how you squeezed yourself into the back of the Jeep (so we could all travel together), setting up a folding chair and looking quite comfortable and photogenic as you waved to cars behind us. When your law school friend saw the photo and got annoyed (or seemed to), I felt I had to take a photo of you on your Juliet balcony so he wouldn't think you were not getting a little pampering too.

And what fun to leave the men back at the house and tour Cruz Bay, we three women, buying Bay Rum soap and cologne and swigging island cocktails at the Beach Bar before staggering up the hill and down the hill, through the woods, and back to the house. Dinner was made by the guys, and later, all of us finished off the rum and danced to somebody's iTunes playlist.

One morning, we were sitting out on the terrace where the peacock often joined us. I had just had a strange and very vivid dream in which two sisters— "Joy" dressed in a yellow gown and "Beauty" in green—came dancing toward me. On the terrace, we spoke about joy, and I was of the opinion that one must create the proper conditions, fertile ground, for experiencing joy when it shows up; you, on the other hand, felt that joy is something that lives inside you that you can recognize and experience and nurture. Which notion is correct? Or are they both? Somehow, I think these two approaches say a lot about the two of us.

I had surgery for a brain tumor twenty months ago. This fact, combined with those initial life expectancy figures of fourteen to twenty-two months, both amazes and terrifies me. I feel good, and at the same time, life can seem so precarious. At some point during this vacation, I realized I had taken a deep, existential exhale and said to myself: *Fuck it! Let me just enjoy whatever life I have left, in whatever fashion that happens to be.* As the poet Jack Gilbert wrote in "A Brief for the Defense," a poem that is both harrowing and beautiful: "We must risk delight."

Love,
Chris

November 27, 2023
New York, New York

SAINT JOHN WAS SUCH A wonderful trip! I'm still amazed that I was only there for two full days and two half days of arriving and leaving—it felt like I'd been immersed in the magic of the impossibly blue water and white sand for much longer. The rum probably helped . . . It was wonderful to meet your friends and see you through their eyes. I loved our girls' walk on the secret path to the gallery owned by the mother of the guy who owns your house, counting the uphill calories burned so we could nosh on some sushi with our rum cocktails. And the hunt for Bay Rum—my dad often wore Bay Rum aftershave, like your grandfather, and it's a scent I associate with love and safety. I haven't used my soap, but it adds a subtle perfume to my drawer. I even had a great time being the kid in the back of the jeep, and your girlfriend was very kind about warning me about upcoming speed bumps.

I think your analysis of our essentially different natures is quite close to the truth, but as usual, you're a bit hard on yourself. I am almost idiotically optimistic at a cellular level; if all prayer comes down to please, thank you, and wow!, I spend a lot of time in wow!

I lost that sense of unquenchable optimism in the first years after Greg's death. I was truly adrift, unmoored, unfathomably bereft over having lost my son, my identity, my understanding of my purpose. The first year of bereavement, for me, was a deeply contradictory time; I felt absolutely exposed, emotionally flayed, but I also felt that

that vulnerability was invisible to the normal humans I was in contact with. One of my friends from the parents' support group refers to people who have not lost children to suicide as "civilians," and I get it; it feels like nobody who hasn't engaged in that particular form of combat could possibly understand you.

Gradually, the deep-seated root of who I am is emerging from the narrow crack of soil between the barren rocks.

Your cycle of emotion, if I may be so bold, seems to often run like this: a vision of ideal perfection that is your dream, a confrontation with reality that mars the dream and can spark a certain petulance, which then provokes guilt, which cycles into acceptance, self-directed humor, and ultimately, evocations of transformative beauty focused on the tiniest of miracles. So, in the end, you find the ideal—you just make yourself work so hard for it!

But I am agnostic about whether there is a correct way to find joy. I do make an effort to notice and pay attention when something just strikes me as beautiful, whether it be the sunlight through a gorgeous Japanese maple at the edge of the Great Lawn on my way to work on a Sunday morning, the wiggle of a small girl dressed as a princess with a sparkly unicorn headband triumphantly leaping with both feet off the last of the scary, windy steps down onto the solid stone floor of the Castle, or the gentle nuzzle of the enormous, silver-coated Great Dane who wanted to get her ears scratched on the path above Turtle Pond. I remember my boys playing in the warm waves on the beach at Agiannaki, the June sun setting after nine p.m., silhouetting the Strophades islands far off on the horizon, and thinking that this memory would stay untarnished forever. It sort of has, even though tinged with sadness. But your joy is no less real or solid if your journey toward it requires your own method of soil preparation. In fact, now that I think of it, the gardener metaphor works very well—different methods and approaches yield the results that the individual gardener is seeking, and the imprint of the creator is what makes it beautiful.

We had a wonderful Thanksgiving, even though Yannis's optimistic (and admittedly vague) estimate of who would show up turned out to be wildly inaccurate. We were only five people, and I had prepared food for about ten—a fifteen-pound turkey, which turned out marvelously, stuffing with sausage and toasted pine nuts, oven-roasted sweet potatoes and garlic puree, more roasted potatoes (I hate mashed potatoes), "slutty" creamed spinach courtesy of Maria Alexia, and Mom's cranberry-orange sauce. Then apple pie, pumpkin pie, chocolate chip cheesecake (Yannis's favorite), bourbon-infused pecan chocolate truffles (Maria Alexia again) . . . lots of leftovers, even after fixing plates for the building staff. One of my work friends came and happily joined in with family stories and reminiscences. A few days beforehand, when Yannis had stopped by, I had gone over the menu with him, strategizing how to make all this in my little apartment kitchen, and he remarked, smiling, that he hadn't seen me excited about cooking for a long time. It's true—I don't give a rat's ass about what I cook for myself and focus on one-pan wonders to minimize cleanup. But this evoked memories of long-ago celebratory meals, where I would plan, experiment, and be delighted to watch people savor food and conversation.

We ate in the building's common room, where there's a big table, and I used both my remaining tablecloths, the longer Irish linen one serving as the base layer and the smaller, everyday one just covering the top. Thrift shop china, plastic glasses and utensils—it was pretty much perfect.

Leaving the Dairy after dusk on Friday, I headed uptown from Columbus Circle to a post-Thanksgiving party hosted by one of my bereavement group moms. As I walked past the sketch artists arrayed just north of Wollman Rink, finishing their final works under the light of the streetlamps, I caught a glimpse of one young man whose stance and facial expression reminded me so much of Greg. For an instant, my heart broke once again.

Love to you,
J

November 30, 2023
Breckenridge, Colorado

O NE YEAR LATER, I AM re reading our correspondence. What am I looking for? I wonder. Maybe an answer to these questions: What has happened in these last twelve months? How am I different? Where do I go from here? May I pose these questions to you?

For now, let me try to find some answers from my own heart.

Last fall, after brain surgery and radiation, and with several more months of chemo ahead of me, I sensed that Alan was watching me. Finally, he asked: "If you begin to think about harming yourself, you'll tell me, right?"

"Of course," I lied, writhing beneath the near-constant electric shock waves of grief and terror I felt in those days. I wonder sometimes if I kept my word because I was too physically and mentally exhausted, too despairing, to order my thoughts and actions into any kind of plan.

This year, in late summer and eighteen months after brain surgery, our mutual friend Maria asked me how I might feel about speaking with a friend of a friend of hers whose husband had just been diagnosed with a brain tumor. When my social worker friend Jake offered me an out, "You don't have to do this, you know," I sat with the request, then understood that I *wanted* to do this.

I corresponded with the wife of this man who is—was—a ship's captain on Lake Michigan. And I came face-to-face while reading her emails with the same terror and disbelief, with the absolute agony of loss she feels that has come out of nowhere and much, much too soon.

In my emails with her over these past weeks, I have tried to be honest, encouraging, and offer emotional and practical help. I witness that I am, today, actually capable of doing this for someone else. I have a similar diagnosis to her husband, but something has changed in the way I view myself and the world. And truthfully, I think a big reason for what I might characterize as a strengthening of steadiness in the face of death is you and I bearing witness to each other and our experience through this writing.

I missed you and our conversations after you'd left Saint John and returned to New York! But our final few days were lovely, if comparatively a bit quiet. And then, Alan and I had a wonderful Thanksgiving with his family outside of Boston, and I had time to reflect on how my thinking, my reality, has changed over the past year. You've made the comment that facing death may be my "superpower," and you've also written how "debilitating loss engenders gentleness, kindness." In no way do I feel like a superhero, but faced with the possibility of my death, I do perceive that Alan and I are often moving through reality on a different plane from those around us.

I don't exactly know how to describe what this experience is like; so far, the descriptions I've come up with sound preachy and judgmental, when actually what I feel is the opposite. In Saint John, as much as I loved being with friends, I became restless at times while sitting with the whole group of us. I had a similar reaction at Thanksgiving dinner in Newton with Alan's family, who I adore and who've been unfailingly supportive of Alan and me.

The experience of Thanksgiving dinner was one of deep comfort, at first, of being a part of this family group, followed by a disconnect, a drifting away, as I perceived the intensity or seriousness each person attached to their likes and dislikes. As if these preferences might protect the speaker behind a wall of certainty.

For fun, I must list some of these Thanksgiving topics, recognizing full well that 1) who am I to judge given that the hot debate around my family's Thanksgiving table when I was growing up was, "Should women be allowed to join the University Club in New York? With their high-pitched female voices! So disturbing to men;" and 2) in the more recent past, I had become just as overwrought about, say, coffee beans as anyone else at this year's Thanksgiving dinner table.

There was, to begin, the horror of processed food (and those who enjoy it), upcoming and carefully curated trips to Europe, Harvard, the political imperative of swapping out gas appliances and cars for the electric versions (How many people can afford to do this? I wondered), competitive biking, the incompetence of others, Harvard again, gym routines, and finally the guilty pleasure of the John Singer Sargent exhibit at the MFA (So popular! And yet so white!).

As the evening continued, as much comfort as I found in being a part of such an educated and opinionated group, I couldn't stop my gradual disengagement. For here we all are, experiencing what may well turn out to be the briefest moment in the history of humanity in which, by sheer chance, we have been born into wealth and relative peace. We have had the privilege of growing up in beautiful and safe surroundings, we've experienced art and ideas and travel, and we are educated and have networks of friends and people who love us. We eat like kings (and queens).

Completely by chance.

I struggle with how it appears, sometimes, that we all believe we have engineered this life—through exercise perhaps, hard work, intellectual prowess, or not eating processed foods—and are therefore superior and, in fact, entitled to the many, many blessings of which we are the recipients. And following this line of reasoning, we can outsmart illness, waning mental acuity, and death through our virtues and obvious superior qualities.

But we can't. We won't. *No One Ever Has.*

At the Thanksgiving table, the talk swirled around Alan and me who were, by turns, kicking each other under the table, eating off each other's plates, and whispering jokes. What I think we both increasingly find of little interest are attempts at directing, judging, controlling—of taking the image we have of ourselves so very seriously. All of this is a burden Alan and I no longer want to carry. How much more valuable to be aware of our vulnerability, our extreme good fortune, and the gift we are to each other? How much more necessary to extend kindness and understanding to the many, many other people who have not experienced our good fortune in life?

Later, when the group of us went en masse to take a brisk post-turkey dinner walk around the neighborhood (counting steps), Alan and I peeled off. As the group accelerated into a competitive death march, Alan and I got lost in the dark wilds of Newton, strolling in our lopsided way with our arms linked just as I recall seeing when my grandparents took a walk.

Finally, today, I got a call from our local bookstore. They had received a letter for me, from a reader of my novel. The letter writer penned this:

> I love this story. This is a story of a second chance that everyone should be able to have. Hope for a future of love and happiness. Thank you for writing this.

Maybe that is where I land, at the end of these twelve months. With thanks . . . and with hope for a future of love and happiness.

> With so much gratitude for you and for our conversation,
> Chris

The Turning of the Year

December 13, 2023
New York, New York

DECEMBER IS HARD. IT'S NOT as awful as it has been, but it's still hard to see and admire all the decorations, to listen to beloved carols, to Handel and Tchaikovsky, to attend holiday parties. The Christmas ornaments are still stored at Mom's house—decorating a tree would be like peeling off a big scab.

Work days in the park are energizing as the shops fill up with holiday shoppers. I was at the Dana on the day last week when we lit a small island of Christmas trees in the middle of the Harlem Meer, and hundreds of children trooped inside to sit with Santa and get their picture taken. Much smaller scale than Rockefeller Center and, in my opinion, more beautiful.

Yesterday involved four different social interactions back-to-back, tiring but energizing too. One of my *koumbares*, visiting from Greece, came over to my apartment and brought me a gift of red amaryllis bulbs just about to open. I had been eyeing amaryllis in stores over the last week or so, a way to mark the season without being full-on Christmas. I had had them in my Athens garden, a gift from Valeria that had multiplied in its planter from one bulb to a dozen over a number of years. This gift just seemed to close that circle—once again, a beloved friend gave me a plant that would grow and (hopefully) thrive and remind me of when I had first learned to appreciate its shape and color. We then went over to the Met, where I toured my *koumbara* around my favorite galleries. The Christmas tree there is once again installed in front of the towering Spanish monastery gateway, decorated just as it has always been since my earliest childhood memories with exquisitely carved and dressed Florentine olivewood figures, including the drunks on the back side of the tree.

Then off to the conservancy holiday party, a wonderful gathering of all the disparate groups that make up the four hundred or so people who care for the park, either by raising its enormous annual budget through donations, caring for its infrastructure and plantings, cleaning up its lawns, woodlands, paths, and promenades, or, like me, giving guidance on "must-sees," bathroom locations, and selling T-shirts and memories to park visitors. Our crew of about eighteen is particularly tight-knit, and I marvel at the fact that a group that ranges in age from twenty-three to eighty-one get along and genuinely enjoy each other's company.

In the early evening, I had coffee with a couple who were my neighbors in Greece for many years—Yannis was classmates with their oldest son, and they had visited us in Agiannaki. They were both raised in New York but have strong Greek roots—I always liked them, but as our boys drifted apart, so did we. We reconnected in a roundabout sort of way—his cousin is a woman I met through her girlfriend, who was in my book club in Athens. It's both lovely and disorienting to meet people you haven't seen in more than ten years, to see the signs of the years (and realize you have also aged!) and yet to experience the same person whose lively intelligence and thoughtfulness attracted you years before. They had just learned about Greg's death—both were forthright about expressing their grief and didn't shy away from the topic or resort to uttering platitudes, something I truly appreciated.

Finally, I had dinner with Harriet and another mutual friend. They are both Upper West Siders but agreed to explore dinner on the other side of the park, so I booked a table at a tiny, quirky French restaurant on Madison in the nineties. Neither of them had ventured out to eat on the Upper East Side in recent memory—New Yorkers are hilariously territorial. We lingered over wide-ranging topics and dessert—the couple at the next table, New Yorkers returning to the city after years on the West Coast, engaged us in conversation, and then gave us the last third of their bottle of wine. I got home a bit dizzy with the wine and the joy of connection.

The holiday whirlwind continues, with both difficult and lovely moments. Our chorus's holiday concert was great fun and mostly a relief. Ours is a no-audition chorus with varying musical abilities, and our director had chosen two demanding works with rapidly shifting syncopated rhythms; it seemed as though every rehearsal descended into chaos at some level, even into early December. It all came together in the final rehearsals and went off beautifully. Yannis has come to realize how much joy singing brings me, and when I expressed concern about our hyper-ambitious spring concert plan—Brahms' Requiem, which I last sang in 1980—he asked, "But you're not thinking about quitting, are you?!" I'm not—even if the prospect scares me. And I love that he sees my happiness and embraces it.

Spending time with Mom in this holiday season is really helpful. She hasn't decorated the house for Christmas since Dad died, and other than gamely making hundreds of Christmas cookies from recipes she has used since Christmas 1962 and mailing them all over the country to her kids and grandkids, she struggles with this time of year. I've told you that my father had an absolutely gorgeous tenor voice and, for many years, was the midnight Mass soloist.

As luck would have it, while she was visiting to attend the concert, I had WQXR's holiday channel playing, and "O Holy Night" came on. Mom choked up. I apologized and explained that one of the reasons I like to listen to this station is that their holiday music is mostly sacred and traditional, and often plays the first carol I can remember hearing—it's a traditional French one, "*Il est né, le divin enfant.*"

And Mom told me why she loved it too, and where she first heard it.

I was born in New York in November 1961, when my father had already received orders transferring him to Verdun, France, for a two-year stint as an Army flight surgeon. He left about ten days after I was born to head off to France, find an apartment, and generally figure things out. Mom had me and my brother Bill, seventeen months old at the time, and was staying with her parents and getting a new passport where, in the photo, she is holding both of us.

My parents were impossibly young—Mom was twenty-four, Dad twenty-seven. After a nightmarish set of flights that took more than twenty-four hours, during which time she ran out of food, milk, and diapers, Mom arrived very bedraggled in Paris. Dad met us, and we drove to Verdun on December 15th. Verdun had never recovered from the cataclysmic damage of the First World War, and the stigma of WWII was still evident all over France—relative poverty, very few men between the ages of thirty-five and fifty without visible war injuries. And Verdun is north and cold.

With the resilience (and maybe blithe ignorance) of youth, my parents were optimistic about furnishing the huge, unheated, empty apartment Dad had found, in which obtaining hot water meant igniting a terrifying gas burner. (My father apparently had most of the hair burned off his right wrist and fingers for the duration.) Dad had scrounged two institutional iron cribs from the base hospital and finagled some other bits of leftover furniture out of the quartermaster. They settled in, essentially camping under fairly Spartan conditions, but ecstatic to be together on this great adventure.

On Christmas Eve, they decided to attend midnight Mass in the Verdun cathedral. Construction on this cathedral began in the year 990, making it (or parts of it) over a thousand years old. Mom remembers walking down a steep hill to the cathedral, her two babies packed into their stroller in multiple layers, and then sitting in a pew, her breath visible, with a gray, bundled-up population, and hearing the men and boys choir sing this carol.

For her, it embodied hope, the grace of having her family together at the start of a great adventure, and the awe of the ancientness of her surroundings. And having her narrate this experience to me sixty-two years later was her gift to me.

In general, I find as much logic and more solace among the ancient gods as I do in church. But there is something lovely, hopeful, and just joyous about celebrating the birth of an infant. No kings, no conquering, no martial imagery, just the reverence of a newborn and the miracle that represents. The traditional Greek Christmas carols are worlds apart from the western canon in musical style, but they contain the same message: "The child is born, the heavens rejoice." The verb used in Greek is related to my favorite word, *agalliasi*—just exuberant, conscious joy. And sharing stories and feelings with my mother softens some of the mutual sadness that the holidays bring.

Wishing you a peaceful, loving Christmas,

J

December 18, 2023
Breckenridge, Colorado

I'D MADE IT THROUGH THE past two months mostly without dwelling on the upcoming, dread-filled date of my next MRI: December 8. But the day itself was as frightening as it always is, even with the usual dose of Valium to keep me from tearing out of my skin.

The results were good. No change from the last MRI.

Despite this encouraging news, I have been hugely out of sorts, taking silent, internal pot-shots at others rather than practicing kindness, gratitude, or acceptance. My first target was the young woman I shared a book signing with near Colorado Springs. Her debut novel was a "Christian-themed" Christmas romance that, in her words, had been "downloaded" to her in the space of one day. Had it not occurred to her publisher, I grumbled to myself snobbishly, that Christmas actually is—*surprise*—Christian-themed? To my annoyance (and envy), this author has been commissioned by her publisher to write two more books.

Then, I had an email from the woman whose husband was diagnosed with a brain tumor in August. She reported on her tireless Google research of treatments and possible outcomes and shared the news that her husband's current life expectancy is at least three to three and a half years. Her apparent confidence that she has any control over her husband's health outcome made me unreasonably angry. But hers is a completely normal response, I reminded myself, she is fighting off her fear with action and a positive attitude.

She and her husband have suffered as Alan and I have suffered. And I hope I responded with kindness and encouragement. To anyone *not* acquainted with brain tumors, this timeline might seem like cause for heart-stopping grief, but in fact, her husband's numbers are good. Better than I was given.

In times of numb despair, a moment will come when the darkness crests. It is as if I am crouching beneath a tidal wave as it towers over me, sucking up all the oxygen. I hold my breath, close my eyes.

And so, the source of my petty anger during this season of goodwill toward all those who seem to have received a "better deal," became clear to me: Next month, January 2024, is month twenty-two since I was diagnosed with a brain tumor and given fourteen to twenty-two months to live.

C

December 21, 2023
New York, New York

MY DEAR FRIEND, I AM aching to hug you and tell you it's all gonna be okay. Even if I have no fucking clue what okay means. You live with a terrible dichotomy—each day is unbearably sweet, but part of that is due to the fact that the days appear to be numbered. Which sucks. But oh, they are so intense, and the hues are so vivid! Even the irritations are magnified, but the moments where Alan hugs you, and a chickadee eats out of your hand, and your marmot looks at you quizzically, and the giant moose thunder across your field of vision—these are eternal.

It's the solstice, and the days are turning. I am going to ask you to do the impossible—ignore the prediction you were given nearly twenty-two months ago. Buy the lottery ticket of hope. Last February, you urged me to see John Lennon's "Imagine" in a different way. So now, *imagine.* Imagine yourself as the medical miracle the neurosurgeons all scratch their heads at happily ten years from now. You're the weird outlier, your particular body chemistry reacted to the latest generation of targeted chemo by killing the glioblastoma cells utterly. Nobody knows why, but they study you. *But* keep experiencing every day as a miracle, even if sometimes the heightened sensitivity is as exhausting as a sunburn, a painful irritation that doesn't let you enjoy anything without letting you know there's a cost.

And forgive yourself for being human, for the accident of birth that put you where you are now, a place of relative privilege and existential dread, for having the occasional twinge of jealousy or even bitterness. My nephew turned twenty-one the other day— my sister's son, Henry, who was a good friend to Greg. My first reaction was a twinge of bitterness—Greg will never have another birthday. But I love Henry, and I love that he remembers his cousin with love, and I forgave myself for the twinge. It's human, and I can be as petty as the next.

I just got off the phone with Yannis, who's leaving for ten days in Greece tomorrow, and already sort of dreading (a) the stress of staying with his girlfriend and her family, (b) dealing with family drama, and (c) missing out on a carefree week in Cartagena with me and my law school friend, with whom he has a wonderful mentor relationship. He knows he's incredibly fortunate in the grand scheme of things, but right now, it doesn't feel like it.

My wish for you is to continue to experience life with heightened awareness and gratitude, to continue beating the odds every two months to the point where the docs suggest that maybe every four months is enough, and to keep writing with me. It's been an unanticipated joy, and one of the things I'm most grateful for.

Much love,

J

December 30, 2023
Breckenridge, Colorado

T HE TIDAL WAVE HAS PASSED. When I wrote to you in early December, all I could conceptualize was this "End Date" of twenty-two months. All I could see was myself crouched beneath this massive swell of dread. And now, somehow, another door has opened, and a new way of understanding things has appeared out of nowhere.

Your response helped me drag myself to my feet. *Use your imagination.* Right? No story about this illness is 100 percent true or 100 percent false. Why not imagine something else? Why not buy the lottery ticket of hope? Even my oncologist, Dr. Ney, warns me against interpreting the data he must give me, if I ask him, as any indication of what the future holds for me personally.

My imagination landed on the story of Hanukkah, with the oil that was supposed to last only for one night but lasted for eight nights. A couple of weeks ago, all I could see was twenty-two months as the end date. Period. Time's up. Today, I still see twenty-two months as the end of something: the end date of a medical data set, the conclusion of a certain period of time in my life of dealing with this illness.

But there is more. The light still burns. There will be the time that comes after. I don't know how to think of this period yet: A new journey that will take me further and deeper into the unknown? Like that corny saying: "When one door shuts, another door opens." But opening on to what? I do not know, but I am walking through.

It has been a tradition among the women on my mom's side of the family to bake these immense loaves of Scandinavian Christmas bread called *bulla*. A weeks-long build-up preceded the baking of these dense braided loaves that involved sourcing cardamom pods and grinding the seeds, slivering almonds, and preparing the kitchen for several days of mixing, rising dough, braiding, baking, cooling. This was in the era of big family gatherings, with all the decorations, fancy tablecloths and china, the rounds of cocktail parties.

This year, my niece Amanda suggested that she and I should bake *bulla*—she in Miami, me in Breckenridge—via Zoom. We agreed it would be fun to continue this tradition . . . but what were we going to do with these enormous loaves that could feed a family of hungry Vikings?

Amanda had been to Copenhagen last spring and ordered "cardamom buns" in a *kaffebar*. We looked up the recipe, and the buns turned out to contain exactly the same ingredients as *bulla*—only we would divide the dough and twist it into individual pastries. The sugary, buttery, cardamom mixture that served as the topping for *bulla*—the loaf version—would now be slathered inside the twined legs of the pastry to create a soft and gooey filling.

Our four-hour Zoom call resulted in sixteen absolutely delicious, sugary, calorie-filled pastries for each of us. How wonderful it seems to me that my niece came up with an alternative so that this tradition could evolve to accommodate time, distance, and changing preferences for sugary, cardamom-laced Christmas treats. Her ingenuity seems to me like a gentle reminder that in ways big and small, even as a door to the past may slide shut, a new door to the future can open.

In addition to cardamom buns, our holiday included a Christmas tree dragged from the woods and enthusiastically decorated by Alan, a days-long visit from good friends and their adorable dog, walks in the mild weather, the magical appearance on Christmas morning of a mother and child moose, and way too much (or perhaps just the right amount of) eating and drinking. After our guests had departed, and the house was once again quiet, I stood outside on the porch, shaking crumbs from my mother's traditional red, green, and blue woven Christmas tablecloth. Above me, in the branches of the aspen tree, a gang of chickadees watched the crumbs scatter with interest.

This morning, the weather has changed. I sit at the dining room table in a house encircled by a screeching twister of wind and snow. The force blows the tall lodgepole pines to near forty-five-degree angles, and I wonder if one will come crashing down on the roof. I watch two ravens flying over the woods, wings pumping and struggling against the blast. Now, suddenly, one solitary raven careens by, a glossy black spirit riding the maelstrom of white.

The Summit County sheriff's office has just sent out a bulletin to *stay off the road!* Ignoring these warnings, Alan has ventured out to secure a celebratory bottle of champagne, and I am alone. As this year comes to a close, I have time on my hands. I can't decide if it is too much or if it is, in fact, just what I need. What I want, but am also reluctant to experiment with, is time to simply sit with difficult emotions.

I want to think about the desire for love and belonging and about fear.

Right before the holidays, I bumped into a local TV/radio producer in a quiet Breckenridge coffee shop housed in a ramshackle Victorian from the old mining days and aptly named Amazing Grace. I had worked with this producer five years ago on a video for the local health clinic. I remembered experiencing him as rather grumpy and impatient. Now, seeing his familiar face after five years when so much has changed for me, I said hello—and then burst into tears.

He sat down with me beside the Grace's cheery woodstove and asked me to tell him what was going on. After listening to my story, he shared with me that his girlfriend was undergoing a very similar and terrifying experience; the two of them have been dealing with her illness for the same amount of time as Alan and I have been contending with mine. As our conversation continued, he opened up to me about his struggle to release his old and outworn anger toward his father—life is just too short. He seemed honestly amazed that I looked so well. He said he admired my courage in pushing forward with life and with projects that are important to me.

Later, at home, I realized how much it had meant to have this face-to-face and completely revealing conversation—no pretense—about both the suffering and the revelations brought about by serious illness. Next, I was startled by how hard it was to sit with this feeling, this longing for honest personal connection. I wanted something sweet to eat; I wanted a glass of wine—something to both prolong the feeling and to act as a distraction from the sarcastic internal voice criticizing me for being so needy of recognition.

But what if I could just sit with this longing, this desire to be heard and respected, along with the anxiety that either it will never be enough or that I shouldn't need it or don't deserve it? Could I just sit with these feelings—whether they embarrassed me or made me feel good, whatever—feel them and be okay with that? Okay with myself?

I am also struggling with the desire to be productive, get things done: writing, preparing my taxes, working on an editing job I have for another writer. Alan's nephews and sister will be visiting soon—I feel the need to be hyper-prepared so that they will think me a good host, and an admirable wife to Alan. So that they might marvel: "All this, despite the fact that she had brain surgery!" In fact, as I write this, I realize how intensely I want people to remark with amazement (now and after I am gone) at all the things I did and accomplished *Even Though I Had Been Diagnosed with A Brain Tumor!*

And what if . . . I did nothing, but was just myself? *What would they think of me?* Today, I try to sit with that anxiety and not fill the day with productive activities to prove I am someone worthwhile, someone who it is still okay and fun to visit. Can I do this? What will happen next?

The bigger, more difficult emotion is fear.

Last night, I spoke to a friend, who sounded as if she had been drinking or crying or both when she told me that one of her dearest colleagues had been diagnosed with lung cancer—completely unexpectedly—and is refusing treatment. Calmly, her colleague has made the decision that she is ready to die. I tried to comfort my friend, to listen. But after the call, I felt as if I'd been lashed to that burning stake of fear. Fear gripped me around my throat, I felt its threat as I hugged myself in bed to try to calm down.

This morning as the storm roars around the house, blocking any plans I had for outside activities, I feel the rising panic of a zoo animal—desperate to escape and afraid to step out of its cage. I sit with this feeling for a while, hyperventilating, and it brings me to tears. Finally, though the fear doesn't disappear, it doesn't feel so overwhelming. Just something that is there.

It seems to me that there is a secret, the shape and texture of which I long to touch, but this secret is always just beyond my grasp: There is a way to hold suffering in our awareness and not be overwhelmed by it. Beauty and kindness and dramatic personal transformation exist side-by-side with terrible loss and pain.

As I struggle to try to understand and accept this, I think about the ravens this morning. Not the two fighting against the wind and snow, but the one who, unresisting, seemed to be riding the storm with fearlessness and utter confidence to wherever the winds may take him.

And now, the clouds have cleared and the sky is blue!

> Here is to a new year of hope and imagination, Jane!
> Love,
> Chris

January 8, 2024
New York, New York

IN A REFLECTIVE MOOD, I went back and read my entry to you from a year ago—astonishing to see how much has changed in circumstances, but not in connection. I read recently that we don't remember the accolades and achievements that the news cycle trumpets from one year to the next, but we remember how we feel, and how others made us feel.

My Christmas day was odd and wonderful. It was supposed to be just Mom and me—Yannis was in Greece and I was working through the twenty-fourth and flying to Colombia for New Year's on the twenty-seventh, so we had a small window. I planned to make Cornish hens, something green, and a rice/grain/lentil mix, just quiet. Then two days before Christmas, the work friend who had joined us for Thanksgiving texted me that her daughter was sick and maybe we could celebrate together? Of course, and in the spirit of "the more the merrier," I invited a couple who are Mom's oldest friends in New York City, and who I consider my godparents, to join us for dessert. They were part of the Verdun cohort and have known me since I was an infant; I had helped their granddaughter with college applications the previous year and had become closer with the whole family.

As luck would have it, they texted me back that a third friend from the Verdun days, who had remarried after being widowed and moved to Israel, was visiting NYC, and maybe we could invite her too. I was overjoyed, since I knew Mom had missed seeing her friend and was very worried about her in Jerusalem.

Since this was turning into a Jewish Christmas, I invited Harriet and her husband Isaac as well. Harriet has heard me talk about these family friends for ages and wanted to meet them. I scrambled to find a kosher bakery nearby; all was set. And the joy of these friends, reuniting with the joy and love of a sixty-two-year friendship, was all I could have wanted for the holiday. Someone said this was *bashert*. (My Yiddish is shaky, so I looked it up; it means "it was meant to be.")

I set off for my third annual holiday with my law school friend—I had picked Cartagena as the destination and was a little nervous since neither of us really knew what to expect. We had a wonderful time. The city is lovely, the weather is hot, the beaches on the nearby islands are beautiful, and the food is memorable. But the best was the company—he is truly a friend of the heart. We've long since gotten over any sexual tension, and we are equally protective of and protected by one another. We were joking that it's like being an old married couple without the resentments and irritations that can build up in a marriage; we talk about everything, and his breadth of knowledge on music, literature, law, and so many other things, is astonishing. He introduced me to a Spanish mystery writer, Arturo Perez-Reverte, who enthralled me (thanks to the instant gratification offered by Kindle). A philosopher and defender of the essential mission of the storyteller: to make the reader ask, "And then what happened?"

On our last day, I was reflecting on the walls of the city. They were built in the seventeenth century when Cartagena was essentially a pirate-infested bastion of the Spanish empire, the transit point for tons of South American loot as well as hundreds of thousands of African souls. That evening, we were having a drink at a bar built on the ramparts, Latin music and colored lights enhancing the atmosphere of wistfulness that always accompanies the last night, and I was telling my friend that I had marveled at the decoration of the gun turrets that dotted the walls. I was drawn to them on my walk early that morning as I watched kestrels swoop and perch on the improbable pineapple finials that decorated the top of each circular tower. These towers were squat, ugly, and functional, with narrow gun slits to enable sharpshooters to pick off the pirates as they approached, firing cannons to breach the walls—and yet, each was topped with a decorative pineapple as an act of defiance or a plea for beauty, or both. I described my meandering thoughts, and he smiled in understanding—what a rare, precious, and wonderful thing it is to be heard and understood.

My inspiration, at the start of the new year, comes from E. M. Forster's *Howards End*: "Only connect the prose and the passion, and both will be exalted, and human love will be seen at its highest. Live in fragments no longer."

Let's connect our fragments, take joy in our connections, and not be afraid to live our passions, even in the shadows of the facts that haunt us.

The happiest of new years, Chris,
Love,
J

Afterword

Where have our lives taken us since we began shaping our year's worth of conversation into this book? The past year has brought changes, some expected, others dreaded, and yet others wholly providential and welcome.

In June of 2024, Chris had to face the news that her brain tumor had recurred—the surgery that followed was deemed successful, and the overall effect on her health has been manageable. She continues to write, walk, travel, and find joy in her life with her husband, Alan. Difficult family relationships have improved, which has been a blessing. March 2025 marked three years since her first diagnosis, meaning that Chris has continued to defy the original prognosis of fourteen to twenty-two months. Jane visited with Chris and Alan a few short weeks after the surgery; she and Chris continue to speak and share their writing on a regular basis.

> *The wind blows through the house. Through our bedroom, the kitchen and living room, and out the open door to the front deck. It has a high-pitched voice as it catapults with glee from room to room, knocking objects from tables, slamming closed unsecured doors. Outside, it climbs into a whirlwind that tosses palm branches and tangles bougainvillea. There is a kind of ecstatic cry*

to the wind, like the voice of the spirit that animates a life. Perhaps my life. All at once, it calms and settles. I listen but now hear no violent, tumultuous sounds; I hear only the whisper of the sea.

Chris, Saint John, January 2025, *journal entry*

In October of 2024, Jane and her son Yannis made a pilgrimage to Ireland and fulfilled Greg's wishes to scatter his ashes in the places that he had designated.

Tomorrow is our last task, the fulfillment of the wishes he had expressed. I've come to see this trip not as closure but as a step in resolution, in knitting him into the place in the family of being and meaning. He is woven into this place so that he is not over, but a part of the fabric of it all.

Jane, October 2024, *journal entry*

Additional Reading

Aristophanes. (n.d.). *The Birds*.

Beck, M. *The Way of Integrity*. Rodale Books, 2021.

de Bernières, L. *Birds Without Wings*. Vintage, 2004.

Brach, T. *Radical Acceptance: Embracing Your Life with the Heart of a Buddha*. Bantam, 2003.

Demosthenes. (n.d.).

Fasano, J. *The Magic Words*. Penguin Random House, 2024.

Forster, E. M. *Howards End*. Edward Arnold, 1924.

Frankl, V. E. *Man's Search for Meaning*. Beacon Press, 2006. (Original work published 1946.)

Freeman, A. (2005). "Planning Ahead Can Make a Difference in the End," *All Things Considered*, June 1, 2005, 12:00 AM ET, https://www.npr.org/2005/06/01/4675953/planning-ahead-can-make-a-difference-in-the-end

Gaiman, N. *Fragile Things: Short Fiction and Wonders*. William Morrow, 2006.

Gilbert, J. "A Brief for the Defense." In *Collected Poems*. Penguin Random House, 2009.

Holbrook, C. "The Serpent Queen." In *Table for One*. Sunroom Studios, 2023.

Markham, B. *West with the Night*. Houghton Mifflin, 1942.

Martel, Y. *Life of Pi*. Knopf Canada, 2001.

O'Donohue, J. *Anam Cara: A Book of Celtic Wisdom*. HarperCollins, 1997.

Oliver, M. *Wild Geese: Selected Poems*. Bloodaxe Books, 2004.

Rush, A. (n.d.). "Two Very Enthusiastic Thumbs Up." Instagram post.

Thich Nhat Hanh. *Reconciliation: Healing the Inner Child*. Parallex Press, 2006.

Thoreau, H. D. *Walden*. Ticknor and Fields, 1854.

Vonnegut, K. "Joe Heller." In *The New Anthology of American Humor*. Penguin Random House, 2005.

Whitman, W. *Leaves of Grass*. Self-published, 1855.

Acknowledgments

This work was born from a private correspondence between two friends. I am immensely grateful to my coauthor, Christina Holbrook, both for the inspiration and for the steadfast, honest, and joyful friendship that deepened over the course of our writing to one another, and for her encouragement to pursue this book as a way of sharing our path to healing with a wider audience.

In the nearly five years since my son's death, I have been held, nurtured and sustained by more friends and family than I can count; naming them here would take pages, so I will settle for thanking some of those who read the manuscript at various points and offered encouragement and advice. These include our agent Peter Garlid, Louise Brockett, Sarah Carroll, Pamela Coravos, Jody Flynn, Mara Flynn, Dorothy Kindred Yewer, Lavender Resnick, Ara Peters, Lucy Tart, Maria Tucci, and many others.

This book would not have been possible without the editing support of Ella Peary and the editorial team at KN Literary Arts, as well as the design skills of Ashley Prine. Finally, I am enormously grateful to my sister, Mara L. Flynn, who listened to us and created the artwork that became our cover.

Jane Flynn

My heartfelt thanks to my coauthor, Jane Flynn, for her patience, kindness, and irreverent sense of humor, all of which have buoyed us on this journey. We've learned so much about ourselves, each other, and about the possibility of transformation under the direst of circumstances. I join Jane in expressing gratitude to our friends, early readers, and publishing advisors.

Love is the best medicine I know. From the early days following my diagnosis and surgery in 2022, friends and family members have rallied, delivering food, cards, and messages of encouragement. Some have travelled across country to help support my husband and me. My Colorado neighbors continue to embody the blessing of community, with offers to hike, share tea and banana bread, or simply to listen.

I have written about some of the medical staff at UCHealth Anschutz, University of Colorado Hospital, who have kept me both alive and sane. I am grateful as well to the many dedicated members of my medical team who have supported me behind the scenes. And I thank my physician and friend Dr. Kathleen Cowie in Summit County for a deeply meaningful partnership that has included ongoing dialogue on topics both medical and spiritual.

To my husband, Alan: Your life, like mine, was forever changed when we learned I had brain cancer. Yet you have remained strong and optimistic, at times carrying us both. You've opened my eyes to the gifts that have come from confronting this challenge together, and from refusing to take one moment of our life for granted.

Christina Holbrook

About the Authors

Jane Flynn

A self-described "serial New Yorker," Jane Flynn was born in Manhattan and lived there through early childhood and again as a young attorney. She grew up in Scarsdale, where she met Christina Holbrook. They bonded as high school seniors over their less-than-stellar field hockey skills, and both attended Wellesley College at the same time.

Jane went on to receive her JD from Harvard Law School, but after a brief career in law, she left family, city, and profession behind, following her future husband to Athens, Greece, in 1990. After learning Greek, she spent the next thirty years raising two sons while navigating the services to support her younger son with autism. She cofounded an autism advocacy nonprofit and later served on the board of the Mediterranean Garden Society while running three coffee franchise outlets in Athens and Piraeus.

Jane returned to New York in late 2020 following the death of her younger son by suicide. She worked in Visitors Services for the Central Park Conservancy for several years and now channels her deep love of Central Park into leading informal tours for friends and volunteering with the Conservancy. This is her first published work.

Christina Holbrook

Born in New York City, Christina Holbrook grew up in Scarsdale, New York, and by her senior year in high school had achieved the pinnacle of her life's athletic success by becoming co-captain of the JV field hockey team with Jane Flynn.

Christina graduated from Wellesley College and moved to New York to find a job in publishing. With an eye for art and photography, and an appreciation for the international travel required for high-end print reproduction, Christina eventually segued into art book publishing, becoming the publisher of The Creative Black Book.

By 2012, corporate life had lost its luster, and Christina quit her job to become certified as a yoga instructor and Reiki practitioner. In 2014, she reconnected with a man who had been her best friend at age fourteen at Scarsdale High School. She moved out to the Rocky Mountains to be with him, and she and Alan Dulit were married in 2018.

Christina has worked as a columnist for the *Summit Daily* newspaper in Colorado, and her short stories have been published in a number of literary journals. *All the Flowers of the Mountain,* her first novel, was published by Sunroom Studiosin 2022 and has received the 2023 Colorado Book Award for Romance, the 2023 IPPY Bronze Medal for Romance, and the 2025 IPPY Silver Medal for Fiction Audiobook.

www.ingramcontent.com/pod-product-compliance
Lightning Source LLC
Chambersburg PA
CBHW021709120626
46545CB00004B/1476